Praise for Unlock The Scribe in You

Unlock the Scribe in You by Dr. Megan Bruiners is not just another book - it is a divine, transformative blueprint uniquely crafted to engage the heart, mind, spirit, and intellect of the prophetic scribe. Dr. Bruiners' insights are real, relevant, and relatable - enriched with clarity and revelation blending biblical principles with practical guidance making this book a supremely powerful prophetic resource. One of the biggest takeaways for me was at the end of chapter one. These seven simple words, "Being vulnerable and transparent are my superpowers" struck me to the core and left me undone. For the first time in my journey as an author, I felt like I finally had permission to own my story and tell it unfiltered.

Between the pages of this prophetic blueprint, Dr. Bruiners delves into a range of themes including embracing your divine assignment, understanding God's vision and purpose, personal growth, spiritual alignment, and more. Together, these themes highlight the unique path of prophetic scribes as we fulfill our divine calling, walk in faith, master stewardship of our gifts and resources, and own our authenticity! One of my favorite themes was mastering stewardship of all our resources in which Dr. Bruiners emphasizes the importance of effectively balancing the pour of our time, financial resources, and spiritual gifts as we walk in our calling.

Unlock the Scribe in You is thought-provoking and imparts prophetic healing, empowerment, wisdom, and instruction. What makes it stand out is its practical approach - it doesn't just inspire, it equips. The steps are non-complexed and easy to follow making it actionable for readers at any stage in their prophetic writing journey.

Through this book, Dr. Bruiners has expanded my imagination providing the clarity, confirmation, and courage I needed to embark on my next move. I highly recommend this book to new, aspiring, and experienced prophetic scribes who are serious about their gift and eager to deepen or expand their prophetic writing abilities. It is a spiritually compatible must-read!

- **Dr. Dionne Greaves**
Hon. PhD in Business Administration and Entrepreneurship
& Hon. PhD in Christian Humanities, Prophetic Ministry
Leader, Business Lifestyle Strategist

Intriguing, Awestruck, Transparency at the Core, Compelling, and Relevant.

Unlock the Scribe in You ministered to my mind, soul, and spirit from the moment I began to read. As I turned each page, I could sense the very presence of Abba Father speaking to my destiny. The magnitude of truth and transparency nestled within the pages of the context pulled me out of a stuck place. The manner in which Megan strategically planned the content for this book was masterful. From beginning to end the tools and strategies provided will be beneficial for the first time or seasoned scribe.

Personally, I could not put this book down. Unlocking the Scribe in You was a clarion call for me to reset, heal, gain greater clarity, and come back to my first love. The level of personal testimonies ministered to the depths of my soul. I could identify with every word written because our stories are similar. I truly believe having this work come across my path was divine. It has given me the courage to complete a few books I started, and determination to begin again. Unlocking the Scribe in You is a nationwide clarion call to those who have been anointed before the foundations of the world as a prophetic scribe. It contains a wealth of practical knowledge and spiritual insight needed to assist scribes in fulfilling their mandate.

I look forward to reading this work again as I personally prepare to reposition myself as a prophetic scribe and birth out God's assignment in the earth for my life.

- Apostle Tonya B. Ratliff
Bestselling Author

If you are a visionary leader who has been called to write and share your God-given message, I recommend not just reading, UNLOCK THE SCRIBE IN YOU, but taking massive inspired action! This book is a guide to help you unlock the potential inside of you and give you the confidence and boldness to write your book and share your message with the world. In this book you will be encouraged to step into your role as a Scribe; a person who communicates the heart of God through revelatory words, and serves as His mouthpiece in their sphere of influence.

Megan is gifted at sharing powerful and prophetic words, and she delivers the same in this book. She encourages the reader to let go of the lies they have been holding on to that may have stopped them from writing their book, and she gives them strategies to stand on the truth of God's Word. She instructs the reader to ditch the scripts and implement Heaven's blueprint to flow in their God-given assignment and spiritual endowments.

If you want to unleash the scribe in you and step into all God created you to be and do, I encourage you to purchase UNLOCK THE SCRIBE IN YOU.

- Nadine Mulling
MBA, Author, Speaker, Podcaster and Founder of the Women
Faith + Business Movement

Unlock the Scribe in You is a book that has arrived at just the right time, though many might feel it has been long overdue. I absolutely needed this book when I decided to start my writing journey 2 years ago. For many years before that I procrastinated and wrestled with finding the time, overcoming doubts and challenges which kept my ideas locked inside of me. The author's writing stirs a desire within you to grab your pen and start writing. I love how she inspires us to dream bigger because there is much more in store for us, and unlocking the scribe in us is a key to help us achieve that reality.

- MICHELLE FARRAR PORTER
Author, Life Coach, Prophet

Unlock the Scribe in You was confirmation for me to dream bigger. Megan not only provides encouragement for our Scribe journey, but also provides frameworks that will help us do the inner work that leads to transformation, deliverance, and an unmuzzled voice. I especially appreciated the guidance on discerning your season and how to break free from negative words spoken. Many parts of Megan's story were relatable, and after reading this book, I feel more equipped and confident to seek out and live out God's purpose for my life in this season.

- PHYLICIA POUGH
Life & Business Systems Strategist,
Founder of The Mom CEO Suite

UNLOCK THE SCRIBE

In You

DR. MEGAN BRUINERS

The Ultimate Blueprint To Courageously Launch Your Book in 90 Days And Amplify Your Authority

Scripture quotations marked (AMP) are taken from the Amplified Bible, Copyright © 2015 by The Lockman Foundation. Used by permission.

First Paperback edition December 2024
Manufactured in South Africa.

Published by Purpose Midwife Pty Ltd
www.meganbruiners.com
Email: MeganCBruiners@consultant.com

Paperback: 979-8-9882200-8-4
eBook: 979-8-9882200-9-1

Disclaimers

The quotes in this book are intended to inspire and encourage readers. The stories included in this book are based on actual events and personal experiences to aid as practical examples for the reader. Neither the author nor the publisher can be held responsible for the use of the information provided within this book. Please always consult a trained professional before deciding to treat yourself or others.

Dedication

This book is dedicated to the individual who doubted their own leadership abilities and the seed of greatness residing inside of them. He is unmuzzling you so your voice can be a beacon of hope. You are seen. You are heard. You are bold and courageous. This is my gift to you.

TABLE OF CONTENTS

PREFACE

Unlock the Scribe in You is an answered prayer to unraveling God's blueprint for your life, book and business. In the fifth month of this year, Holy Spirit whispered to me in a still voice, you need to birth the book I'm imparting to you. At first, I thought it was the prophetic visionary in me that wanted to take on yet another task because it sounded like a fun idea. I typed the vision out and stored it electronically to revisit it after receiving more clarity on how to proceed. One month after my encounter, I received an instruction from the Lord to act now or the window of opportunity would close to write the book in His appointed time. I realized that it was my new assignment and paused some of my projects in obedience. Immediately after I gave my YES, I got divine inspiration for my book cover, chapter outline and overall theme in less than one hour. The manuscript was completed in twenty days while raising two toddlers, with a fully written out marketing plan that would position me to steward the book well. My husband understood the assignment and supported this timely message I was entrusted with.

There is a great possibility that you haven't been asking God for BIG things because that's what you've been taught growing up. By default, we've been wired to play small and downplay our gifts because we don't fully grasp who He has called us to be. When you're a Faith-driven leader on a mission to influence change, your message will undergo a pruning process. Suddenly, you doubt your capabilities, confused about who you're supposed to serve, and God's voice is being drowned out by the noise. When you stop to pause and reflect, you'll realize that your time in the secret place was replaced with busy schedules and frameworks that pushed you off rhythm. You settled for less because that felt familiar. Well, that season is in the past. When we mimic someone else's formula, it's an identity issue because we have not yet discovered our own unique methods.

The revelation I received is that I was running with someone else's blueprint which wasn't designed to propel my destiny and the abundance that was promised to me. It was not in alignment with my Kingdom values. God disrupted everything that wasn't from Him so I could rebuild it again following His blueprint for my life. He healed my brokenness and revived me again so I could get back into alignment to build with new zeal. This is the same blueprint He wants for you, so that you're not lured into being a carbon-copy of someone else. It will take courage to unlearn old mindsets as you submerge yourself into being vulnerable as a leader. This bold step will reignite the vision for your book so that you can become unstuck and confidently walk out your Kingdom calling. *Get ready for the overflow!*

INTRODUCTION

I invite you on this exhilarating adventure of partnering with God as He unlocks the Scribe in You so you can launch the book He called you to write. If you're a visionary leader or prophetic person who desires to be bolder and more courageous, you're in for a treat. I have cracked the Kingdom code to finishing your book using heaven's blueprint so you can finally ditch the old scripts and amplify your impact. However, you have a role to play so that the promise can come into fulfillment. The overcomer stories outlined in this book were designed to activate the seed of greatness inside of you. The grace I've experienced while excavating the gold in my story, which spans over forty years, reminded me of all the challenges I've conquered. I felt the conviction from Holy Spirit that our voices have been muzzled and our stories are buried under doubt and fear of rejection. There was a burden to make haste so I could shout my message from the mountaintops because it will release a sound into the atmosphere that will attract a new remnant of visionaries that's arising. They will flow authentically as they make room for Him to move and unlock their voice. The transparency throughout this book was curated purposefully to lead an open conversation by processing the fears that's keeping you in a holding pattern so you can heal from past failures.

The prophetic prayer journaling prompts will awaken a deeper intimacy with God so you can yield to His voice in this new season. If you've been struggling to prioritize your time so you can write in your authentic voice, the practical steps will lay the foundation for building an online brand or growing your existing business by leveraging the book.

I would do this again in a heartbeat. My encouragement is that you should not skip any steps and to set time aside to do the inner work that is required before the signature framework produces results. He is giving you discernment so that you can move forward in faith.

Then he said to me, "This [continuous supply of oil] is the word of the LORD to Zerubbabel [prince of Judah], saying, 'Not by might, nor by power, but by My Spirit [of whom the oil is a symbol],' says the LORD of hosts. (Zechariah 4:6)

The five books I've written before birthing this one prepared me to unwrap a deeper revelation in my personal experiences with people-pleasing, setting healthy boundaries and unmasking your purpose. As the reader you will be immersed into a place of rest and self-introspection to finally execute God's purposeful strategies for your life, book and business. You are being established as an author so you can finance the Kingdom of God and be a conduit for the message He wants to birth through you. As a trailblazing leader this is the beginning of a beautiful exchange of surrender, trust and becoming. If you're building a personal brand or transforming lives with your marketplace message, this book will be a unique tool to amplify your message so your dream audience can connect with your story.

Here's a breakdown of the three parts:

In Part One we will embark on a thought-provoking journey of **re-discovering** your purpose so that you can become rooted in the core identity of who you are in Christ. Renewing your mind with the truth of God's word forms the crux of obliterating the lies of the enemy as you unmask false belief patterns and emotional soul wounds that are hindering your progress. You will also be equipped with the five Kingdom Strategies to break free from negative words spoken over you and releasing the power of rejection. As you get clarity on your assignment and which season you're in, your passions will be reignited so that you're positioned to write the book God called you to birth in this season.

In Part Two we **unlock** God's blueprint to launch your book courageously over the next 90 days by implementing our proven ten-step process. Receive prophetic insights to embrace your authenticity and anointing as you flow in your gifts in the marketplace. We delve into the four action keys to shift your mindset from feeling powerless to becoming a fearless thought leader that influences nations with your transformative story.

In Part Three you will get my Bestseller secrets and five-figure framework to build a Signature Kingdom Author brand beyond launching the book that's been designed to skyrocket your business. Live out your message courageously with seven faith pillars that will propel you to **uncover** the hidden treasures inside of you. Get ready to be **unleashed** into your calling as a Scribe so you can amplify your authority and step into your prophetic destiny.

My heart for you is to be who God created you to be and not live your life to please people, but be driven by purpose. You are wonderfully made and only putting the pieces of your story together so that serves as a lighthouse to many. Whatever you do, promise me you'll never dim your light to fit in so that you can experience the more He predestined for you. *Now, go write that book already!*

In His Service,
Dr. Megan Bruiners
Prophetic Book Consultant, Kingdom Publisher & Hon. PhD in Christian Humanities.

WORD OF ENCOURAGEMENT

"You can't solve someone else's problem through your writing if you haven't quite figured out who you are."
~Dr. Megan Bruiners

Part One

CHAPTER ONE

What is my purpose?

I was in an identity crisis up until my late twenties when I started to receive divine revelations of what I've been created to do on the earth. For the most part it felt like I was in a maze as I always craved validation and approval from others because of my insecurities. Layers of false identity kept me in bondage from who God uniquely created me to be. Pleasing people was my drug of choice. My voice felt muted as a young adolescent and my leadership potential was buried by my lack of confidence. I didn't start my journey being bold and courageous because of the fear of making mistakes. The freedom to fully express myself was non-existent so it was easier to stay in the comfort zone where no one could see you.

Feelings of insignificance and unworthiness will lead you to abort your destiny. As an overcomer of approval, addiction, shame, and rejection it was a daily decision to lay it all down at the altar while uprooting generational patterns in my bloodline.

In my first book that launched in 2020, *Unmasking Purpose: A Guide to Overcoming Addiction and Discovering Your Purpose*, I detailed my personal testimony with breakthrough strategies of how you can victoriously live out a purpose-driven life amidst the challenges.

What was yours? It could be grieving a loved one, overcoming an addiction, surviving church hurt, unforgiveness, demystifying shame, or battling rejection. The plan of the enemy is to derail you emotionally, so you don't receive a revelation of the power that resides in you. When you focus on the pain you lose sight of the promises of God which are Yes and Amen. We are not denying that the crushing process wasn't excruciating, but encouraging you to trust that the author and finisher of your faith knows all things will work out for your good. When we live our lives to please people we make an idol of their opinions instead of pleasing God and walking in obedience.

I remember while curating one of my Multi-author book projects that one of the leaders questioned my marketing strategy even though it was the first time she was featuring as an author and I had done it multiple times. I was collaborating with dynamic women from across the globe and the vision I received from the Lord was clear. He has given us the authority and grace to execute what He has imparted to us because He sees the bigger picture. After staying true to my convictions, the Lord revealed her motives and that everyone is not your destiny helper. Destiny killers are very real therefore we should discern who we go into partnership with.

I believe that the Lord is stirring the hearts of His chosen vessels to be bold and courageous as they are called to write in this season. This can only happen when they know who they are in Christ beyond the roles and titles they've been given to steward. When you don't understand that your identity precedes your actions, you will flame a misconception that your works, accolades, behavioral patterns, and accomplishments complete you.

The disappointment leading up to you being awakened to purpose was not in vain. It molded you into the resilient leader you've become. The deeper your intimacy is with God, the more clarity you receive pertaining to your identity. There are hidden gems waiting to be unlocked on the inside of you. Your purpose was never lost nor is it something outside of who you are. It's the reason for your existence. You may not be fully functioning in it yet or unable to see the bigger picture. When we go through hardships there is a refining process that takes place. Fulfilling your purpose is not based on works, but stepping into what God already predestined for you by faith.

Paul wrote in Romans 8: 28, 30, '*And we know [with great confidence] that God [who is deeply concerned about us] causes all things to work together [as a plan] for good for those who love God, to those who are called according to His plan and purpose.*

And those whom He predestined, He also called; and those whom He called, He also justified [declared free of the guilt of sin]; and those whom He justified, He also glorified [raising them to a heavenly dignity].'

When your heart posture is right you can rest assured that whatever decision you make will turn out for your good. *Living out your message on purpose requires courage because you will be tested.* He graced you for the assignment. Seasonal assignments are small tasks that prepare you for your purpose and calling. Therefore, walking in obedience is a daily commitment.

Being led by our emotions and not being spirit-led takes us out of alignment with our God-given assignments. You're not called to everyone and don't owe anyone an explanation of what the Lord is doing in your life. The fastest way to get burnout as a leader is to be consumed by busyness and use all your energy to meet everyone's needs. If you're saying YES to everything then it's inevitable that you're saying NO to the most important thing that needs your attention. When you understand that your unique mandate goes beyond church gatherings, your corporate job and life groups, then you'll dream bigger.

As a multi-faceted visionary leader, I've learned to ask God to activate dormant gifts that will empower me to complete my assignment in my role as a prophetic book consultant. In the Kingdom of God, sonship precedes the work we do and speaks to who we are being without the titles. When you write your story from this royal position, you will not allow your shortcomings, inadequacies, and past failures to overshadow your creativity and ability to flow in your spiritual endowments so you can complete your assignment.

Many trailblazing leaders fail to execute their book ideas because it's unfamiliar territory which stretches them to move differently. Listen, there's no blueprint for what you've been assigned to do. Scribe, you are the blueprint!

The Great Awakening

In 2018 I was awakened to my gift of writing while attending a Masterclass for aspiring authors even though I hadn't quite connected the dots to my purpose. Only two years later the light bulb went on. Every failure, betrayal, disappointment, rejection, unplanned detour, and divine disruption prepared me for where He was calling me too. It didn't only happen to me, but for me. That was the missing piece for me. I was looking for an outward experience when there was an internal crisis raging on the inside. I was at war with myself and the truth seemed daunting. After many prophetic journaling sessions and spending time in the secret place, God highlighted the areas He wanted me to heal in. We are more than overcomers and the responsibility rests on us to work through any unaddressed issues that arise so that it doesn't hinder you as a Kingdom Scribe.

While writing about my own grief journey in my very first book it was an outlet to release my emotions and come into agreement with His plan amidst the pain. Surrendering your internal battles to God is one of the best decisions you can ever make because He is the Great Physician. Only then can you have dominion in your sphere of influence. Only four years after our global crisis, during the time of a spiritual reset, the message that Holy Spirit convicted me to write prophetically makes sense. We are living in the era of a great awakening now.

Sometimes the message He instructed you to steward is not for now, but for what's coming or an appointed time. We are being spiritually awakened to the schemes of the enemy and can no longer be double minded about who we are, who we're called to, and what we're supposed to do. We must come out of hiding and be the light in this dark world. One of the ways to do this is to unmuzzle your voice and share your authentic story. I also understand that there are parts of your testimony that's not for everyone therefore discernment is necessary as you co-author with Him. I will be deep diving into key strategies of how you can give an account of your personal story gracefully in the latter part of this book. When we live our lives for people, we will seek their approval which is contrary to the word of God.

When you get this revelation and position yourself to steward the message He has given you well, you will get the clarity around why it was necessary to navigate your way through the wilderness seasons. You wouldn't have seen your resilience, inner strength, tenacity, and pioneering spirit. I can say without a doubt that you're not satisfied with the status quo and desire more of God. *He wants you to walk in the abundance He has for you more than you know.*

Settling is not your portion. If I didn't believe my story was powerful, I would have lived an average life below my maximum potential. Unfulfilled. Distracted. Blending in.

Discerning your season

You have entered a new season where outdated strategies will no longer serve you. You've never been here before, that's why it feels foreign to you. Some of the most frequently asked questions I get from prophetic leaders in my online author academy are, *'When do I move to take action and when should I wait on God'* and *'How do I know which book I'm supposed to write first.'* When you are not plugged into the Source you will be confused about your next move. More than likely you have many voices that have your ear when you should be listening to His voice alone.

There are sowing seasons that will place a demand on you (based on Kingdom principles) to sow seeds into people, places and environments to advance the Kingdom of God. It won't bear fruit immediately and your attitude will be tested as you trust the process. The words you speak over yourself and the people surrounding you in this season is pivotal for your growth. If you just started a business and you get frustrated because you're not seeing results over the first two years you can kill your seed that was planted. Unforgiveness and offense also destroys your seed and dilutes your message because it is out of the heart that the mouth speaks. There is life and death in the power of the tongue. If you're a giver you must apply self-control when everyone has an expectancy on you for financial dependency, so you don't deplete your resources. We need to manage and steward it correctly.

In the next 'cave' or wilderness season the seed needs to be *nurtured* so that you can reap what you've sown when harvest time comes. During this time, you are waiting on God for the next instruction as *you rest in Him.* You're not striving in your own strength and not shying away from the internal work while uprooting the worries of the world. He has given you a sound mind, therefore, you do not have to be anxious about the outcome. You will be pruned and pushed out of your comfort zone so that you can withstand the weight of your next assignment. This is more often the space where He calls Scribes to be bold and courageous even when they don't feel that way. Then suddenly you have a desire to write your story, but trying to figure out all the missing pieces. It may seem like you lack clarity and are unsure if you should wait or go.

What I've discovered from working with authors on a global platform is that He is now inviting you to act while surrendering what you think the book should be about and focus on the message that is needed in this hour. What that looks like to you could be rebranding your brand/business, showing up consistently in your community, being authentic, and solving the immediate problem of the individuals assigned to you in the marketplace. Your unique message is buried in the story you're afraid to tell. You will only get clarity when you write down the vision and make it plain. Not every idea would be for right now if you're a creative, but you still need to document it and come back to it later as you build it out. You will never feel ready to implement the divine strategy He gives you; it must happen by faith especially when you fail to see the results. There should be an expectancy. *Doubt is a destiny killer.*

In your reaping season you must reap what you have sown. It's a spiritual law. If you're a first-time author, then the writing process may feel overwhelming. There are belief patterns working against you that the book must be fully funded before you get started. You're overly cautious because you see it as an expense, instead of a good investment. When we say that He makes provision for the vision then our faith needs to match that. If you've grown your business or ministry and are pursuing authorship as a step of obedience to be a Kingdom financier, you have to be all in. Avoid the trap of using words, *'I can't afford it'*, or *'I don't have the time to write.'* That's exactly what you'll receive. When you have a gameplan you can set it up in a way that you get back a return of investment before the book is published. If you've authored many books but solely depend on the sales, you miss out on the opportunity to transform lives beyond the publishing of the book. I will elaborate in the latter chapters.

In your harvest and abundance season you can expect to see the fruit of your labor. You're living in the overflow while replenishing for the next season. You're confidently walking out the movement He entrusted to you. The prophetic words spoken over you have come to fruition and you're living in it. It's crucial that you create boundaries and protect your peace when everyone wants to be connected to you and the anointing on your life. Some relationships are transactional and not everyone will celebrate you. Stay focused on your goal. Alignment with the right destiny helpers will accelerate your next level growth. You will be tested. Stay humble and keep your heart pure.

You're not dreaming big enough

The Lord had to deal with me whenever I would shrink back and play small. He reminded me of my childhood dream and silent prayers that I forgot about. It's the Father's heart for us to dream and ask for big things. Your imagination is one of the most powerful tools you have when co-creating with God when outlining your book or designing your cover art. You must visually see it before you can bring it to life. When you dare to dream you come into agreement with what He ordained for you. What would happen if you embraced the scribal anointing and asked for the spiritual gifts that you aren't flowing in yet? You will be unstoppable and bold to speak His heart in the boardroom, a corporate gathering, or in your children's kindergarten class.

Your dream may be to buy huge hectares of land off the grid to build a restoration haven for destitute ministry families, to provide safe homes for abused women, or to create a sanctuary for single moms who have backslidden because of addiction. Let's keep it real, you need finances to support these movements. *He is able to do more, exceedingly and above all that you could've asked for, but you have to see Him as a good Father that wants to give you good gifts from above.*

Whenever God answers your prayers, dream bigger, because what you've experienced thus far is only a drop in the ocean of what's to come. But you should believe that it will come to pass in His kairos time. In your pursuit of growing in intimacy with Him you spontaneously discover facets of yourself you never knew existed. If hope deferred makes the heart sick, then something killed the fire that was once in you. You can reignite your passions by surrounding yourself with purpose-driven leaders, making time for the things you love, and releasing individuals who are holding you back from evolving into the person you're supposed to become.

My prayer is that you will re-discover your identity to the core and be unmoved when you are misunderstood or face rejection. As an encourager it comes naturally to me to motivate others, and I genuinely want to see you win. Being vulnerable and transparent are my superpowers. I'm drawn to authenticity where you don't have to fake it to make it. That's the beauty of being you, unapologetically. Scribe, it's time to pick up that pen and dream again.

JOURNAL PROMPT: Take 10-15 minutes in your day to prophetically prayer journal and talk to the Lord. You can read the word and play soft worship music in the background if you feel led to do so. Ask Him to revive a long-life dream in your heart or awaken you to your purpose. Listen to what Holy Spirit wants to say to you and write down the spontaneous thoughts that flood your mind. He may give you a particular scripture, encouragement, or guidance for your next steps. The more time spent doing this activity will increase your intimacy as you grow spiritually. Record the date and year that you've asked the question so that you can go back to it when the Lord answers your prayer.

SCRIPTURE FOR REFLECTION

"Therefore if anyone is in Christ [that is, grafted in, joined to Him by faith in Him as Savior], he is a new creature [reborn and renewed by the Holy Spirit]; the old things [the previous moral and spiritual condition] have passed away. Behold, new things have come [because spiritual awakening brings a new life]." ~2 Corinthians 5:17

CHAPTER TWO

Who said that?

This is a question I ask whenever I'm coaching new clients which takes them back to a particular event in their childhood or adult life that opened the door to fear, insecurities and feelings of not being good enough. It could also be words you've spoken or inner vows you've made with yourself. When I started in entrepreneurship a few years ago there were many thinking patterns that I found myself repenting of. One of the foundational scriptures used to replace the lie with the truth was based on Romans 12:2 where Paul wrote, *'And do not be conformed to this world [any longer with its superficial values and customs], but be transformed and progressively changed [as you mature spiritually] by the renewing of your mind [focusing on godly values and ethical attitudes], so that you may prove [for yourselves] what the will of God is, that which is good and acceptable and perfect [in His plan and purpose for you].'* A complete mindset shift was necessary to steward my business well. My thinking was transformed from lack to abundance. From grinding to resting in His grace. From being anxious to abiding in His peace. From striving to being rooted in my identity in Christ.

As you grow in relationship with the Lord and co-create your book with Him, you will find that beliefs you held onto tightly for so many years muted your voice. Perhaps it started all the way back in kindergarten when the teacher spoke words over you that made you doubt your ability. It could've been a parent who destroyed your confidence through their action, hateful words and rejection while growing up as a teenager. You may have endured bullying in high school or in the workplace that caused you to become introverted and incapable of expressing your emotions. We can breakdown a myriad of examples that may have contributed to past trauma or feelings of unworthiness that is delaying your breakthrough, however, the focus for this chapter is to give you practical Kingdom keys as you trust Holy Spirit to highlight any soul wounds so that you can boldly walk out the mandate He has given you. *Unhindered. With a posture of surrendering what you don't fully understand yet.*

Our words carry weight in the spiritual realm and have the power to break someone down or edify them. *'Death and life are in the power of the tongue, And those who love it and indulge it will eat its fruit and bear the consequences of their words.' (Proverbs 18:21)*

Just imagine walking around with a heavy backpack filled with every stereotype, label, word curse, opinion and self-sabotaging words ever spoken over you. It was not designed for you to carry on your own because His yoke is easy, and His burden is light. Here are five keys you can implement to break free from words formed against you to kill, steal and destroy.

Five Kingdom Strategies to break free from negative words spoken

Strategy One – Cancel the negative words and come out of agreement with it

Nullify and cancel the words spoken over you and deal with it *immediately* so that its effects are powerless and have no hold over you. This also applies to the words that you are not aware of that's spoken against you. It's in your best interest to be proactive instead of reactive and commit to dealing with those word curses.

In Isaiah 54:17 it says, *"No weapon that is formed against you will succeed; And every tongue that rises against you in judgment you will condemn. This [peace, righteousness, security, and triumph over opposition] is the heritage of the servants of the LORD, And this is their vindication from Me," says the LORD."*

Strategy Two – Manage your emotions

Repent of your own words that you've spoken over yourself in anger or frustration when being led by emotions. You may not have thought about the consequences of your words in a heated argument with your spouse or children, but it was still released into the atmosphere. These are accusations that the enemy has against us because we will reap what we've sown, and we are not exempt from this biblical principle. Make it a daily habit to ask Him to show you areas you neglected to deal with in your own life so that it doesn't hinder your assignment as a leader. Desire to be led by the Spirit of God by surrendering your way of doing things. Our children model our behaviors and we teach them how to manage their emotions by being the example.

Strategy Three – Identify the pattern in your generational line and heal from the soul wounds

If you grew up in a family line where negative words were used to hurt you, then the same principle can be applied as mentioned in strategy one. You don't have to emulate what you've been exposed to because you have the blueprint, which is the word of God, so you can live victoriously. Find a trusted accountability partner on your journey to wholeness. As you write the chapters of your book as a Scribe you will encounter emotional roadblocks which you have to work through. He will use your weakness and vulnerability as you capture your powerful story and give you the divine strength to finish what you've started. There will be a grieving process of who you used to be and a rebirth of who you are about to become. You will have the opportunity to journal your thoughts in the latter part of the book. Don't hold back and write it all down. He has something new for you. *Receive it.*

Strategy Four - Getting offended is a choice

You may get tempted to get offended and it will be a decision you have to make to pick it up or leave it alone. *It's a trap.* All of us have been offended at some stage, but we are instructed to forgive those who have hurt us on purpose or unintentionally. When we don't we put up a fence between us and the person who offended us. Nothing comes in and nothing goes out. We were not created to live with strife and bitterness in our hearts and can be likened to drinking poison and expecting that individual to die from it. It also hinders our prayer life because our hearts are not pure. Be mindful that the root offense can lead to being resentful when someone doesn't meet our expectations. If you never heard the words, 'I love you' or 'I'm proud of you' from your parents while growing up, it can grow into bitterness when you haven't dealt with the offense in your heart. When someone doesn't communicate what you've longed to hear, it is more subtle than an individual expressing it to you in words. Catch the thought at its onset and ask yourself if there is any truth in it. Be sober and alert when the emotion does arise. Deal with it accordingly.

Strategy Five – Speak life and bless those who curse you

Walking this one out can only be accomplished when being led by Holy Spirit. The moment you realize that it's not about you and that the fight is not against flesh and blood, you will pass the test when you allow God to vindicate you. This is the greatest indicator that you're ready for next level growth as a visionary leader. *How well do you manage the pain of betrayal or slander?* Supernaturally tap into the fruit of the Spirit in Galatians 5:22-23 as He turns everything the enemy tried to use for your demise into good. This posture will set you free to flow in your writing and to use the crushing experience to glorify God with your story.

> Two of the biggest reasons pioneers don't birth the book inside of them are because of what people have said or what they've said to themselves. Rejection and shame are silent killers, and He wants to set you free from them.

Breaking off the power of rejection

I want you to see my story and the transparency I'm about to share as permission that God can use you too when you make yourself available. I lived in shame for thirteen years of my life before being delivered from it without anyone laying hands on me. I was desperate for a change. I experienced self-sabotage and rejection up until my late twenties while believing people's opinions mattered before I ever got an opportunity to utter a word. I was petrified of making mistakes and being judged. *He still chose me.*

I thought I dealt with rejection until I pivoted in my online author business which pushed me out of my comfort zone as I reached out to Kingdom leaders on social media. For the enrollment of my first International Multi-authored book project I curated, *Just Say No*, I interviewed 62 Faith-driven entrepreneurs to feature as an author. The amount of no's on the interest calls was discouraging, but I pushed through despite feelings of inadequacies. While I was looking at the numbers, He was shaping me while increasing my faith. My determination paid off after onboarding fourteen dynamic women globally to feature as co-authors and taking the book all the way to

#1 International Bestseller on Amazon in three countries. I faced the fear of rejection head-on in this project while my leadership and entrepreneurial skills were developed. I was all in because one of my values is not to do anything half-heartedly. I'm so glad I refused to settle and focused on the bigger vision He showed me. It turned out that moving forward courageously through unfamiliar territory is how He broke the power of rejection off me. *I was merely being obedient.*

Once we renew our minds daily through reading the word, we can take thoughts and imaginations captive before it takes up residence in our mind and becomes a stronghold. It's a daily decision we must make. If there's a history of rejection in your bloodline that wasn't dealt with, you are next in line to stop the cycle as a generational curse breaker. There may be events you suppressed and dissociated with causing you not to work through them. When you look at the pattern in your family line you will begin to identify that you're not the only one that experienced rejection or shame. True freedom is when it no longer has a grip over you and your God-given destiny. I'm confident that as you continue to seek Him daily that you will identify your triggers and guard your heart above all things. That you will experience restoration in the area that your trust has been broken and get back on the wall to finish your assignment. I know this may sound counter-active to what I just spoke about, but rejection saved my life. I would not be the leader I am today if my character wasn't tested. *Ridiculed. Betrayed. Slandered.*

I've worn all the t-shirts. It reminds me of a client I fired after she attacked my character on a mission to sabotage a book project we collaborated on. She went as far as to say that she wouldn't even be interested in the strings of my shoe and lashed out because she wanted the outcome a certain way. I recognized the spirit behind her lashing out and gave it to the Lord who vindicated me. Months later she emailed me and apologized for her behavior. I held no grudge against her because I understood my assignment at the time. The enemy's plan is for you to stay offended. *Pass the test the first time so you don't have to take it again.*

When you follow God's blueprint for your life you will never fail. You have been graced for it.

Believing in your message

What belief-shifting message did He give you to steward? If you're building a spirit-led business, you need to believe that the services you offer transform lives before anyone will. You've been given the ability to take dominion in the marketplace with your story. If your flame was taken out because of circumstances out of your control, just know He can reignite it. Get your passion back. Be filled with unspeakable joy again. Overflowing with peace that transcends all understanding. Make a fresh commitment to the vision He gave you for your book, business, family, emotional well-being and spiritual growth. Don't overthink it. Step into the new season He has for you as you continue to remove layers of false identity. I've encountered many counterfeits in the entrepreneurial space and ministry that looked good from the outside but wasn't from God. Their assignment was to replicate or imitate the anointing of God so they could deceive His chosen vessels from fulfilling their destinies. When you write your message as a Scribe from a position of spiritual authority you are authorized to take territory in the sphere of influence He has called you to. It may be media, podcasting, publishing, blogging, consulting, speaking, or writing books for a global audience.

The mindset shifts of transitioning into becoming a thought leader will demand you to think differently and inevitably set you apart from only seeing yourself as an author who merely wants to tell their life story. If you've read thus far, I'm convinced you're an eagle with a vision so big that it scares you. He entrusted it to you because you have the capacity to birth what He showed you. Some of the pitfalls I've seen many authors make is to downplay the anointing on their life and not get visible before the book is published. One of the ways to increase your visibility is to get on other people's platforms or go live on yours. Speak about the things you've overcome and how it ties into how you're empowering your community today. You're an inspiration to someone you haven't met yet. We will delve more into this in chapter six.

I never understood why I was led to host my own tv show for an entire year while experiencing technical issues and an unstable internet connection while interviewing trailblazers from across the globe. It was my training ground. I created content effortlessly and forged authentic relationships with women from all walks of life which was priceless. One of the tv shows I hosted, *Amplify Your Voice*, streamed in 200 million households in the top three countries which were USA, Canada, and UK. Showing up weekly to virtually record content made me resilient. I pushed through because I believe what the Lord imparted in me is not for myself, but for that one person who desires to be in alignment and walk out the call of God on their life. I'm now in the process of launching my own audio podcast that I've placed on hold for more than a year because the timing is right. Not surprisingly, I fell in love with listening to inspirational stories and creating a space for pioneers to amplify their voice.

Authorship is only the entry level to your next wave of endless opportunities. He has so much more for you. As your destiny helper, my assignment is to pull out the gold inside of you over the upcoming chapters. Two of the most common questions I get from aspiring authors and prophetic leaders in my community are, '*How do I write my story without hurting anyone?*' and '*What qualifies me to write a book people will read?*' Firstly, the purpose of you writing about your personal experiences is not to expose anyone, but to lead the conversation authentically so that you can be the voice to others that need the tools and encouragement that you flow in naturally. The power resides in what you've overcome and the steps you took to overcome it. When you partner with Holy Spirit and get accountability from the right mentor to guide you through the process, you will receive the impartation on what the focus point should be and who it's targeted for based on the season you're in. *Remember, you're writing your truth in your authentic voice.* And of course, you also have access to my proven blueprint for launching your book courageously in 90 days. It's imperative that you apply wisdom and discern which parts of your testimony to include if you're working on a non-fiction book, devotional, or a series of short stories. I would encourage you to get clarity around what the intention of the book would be before moving forward so that you heal from a particular event that surfaces through prayer journaling and seeking godly counsel. He may lead you to take another direction and invest your time in creating a leadership book first to showcase your expertise with glimpses of your story.

In reference to the last question, *God qualifies the called.* In some capacity you've already mastered an area in your field. Think about it. You received revelation and insight into what your clients need, but need the steps to implement it. Visionaries love creating and can get caught up with too many ideas without taking deliberate action. That's why I'm here journeying with you. If you've written books before and have not yielded the fruit of your labor, there's multiplication waiting for you so that you can advance the Kingdom of God. You must believe it to your core.

In the next chapter we're getting rid of the distractions so that you can get a greater understanding of your scribal anointing. Are you ready?

JOURNAL PROMPT: Take 10-15 minutes in your day to prophetically prayer journal and talk to the Lord. You can read the word and play soft worship music in the background if you feel led to do so. Ask the Lord to reveal any areas that you still need to heal from, and work through the emotions. Record the date and year that you've asked the question so that you can go back to it when the Lord answers your prayer.

WORD OF ENCOURAGEMENT

"Speak it, until the people that understand your language show up."
~Apostle Melvin Thompson III

CHAPTER THREE

Who's my tribe?

It took me a minute to discover who I'm called to serve because of all the noise in the online space. As a postgraduate student I was accustomed to doing qualitative research for my thesis in which I used the data to formulate the outcome of my hypothesis. If that sounds foreign to you, imagine my bewilderment when I was told to 'speak the language' of my clients when marketing my services. I struggled to wrap my mind around it even though it sounded so simple. Surely there was another approach I was missing that a Master's degree couldn't fix.

We have begun to sound robotic with the 'I help' statements and 'knowing your niche' scripts that we've lost our authentic voice as Scribes and spirit-led entrepreneurs. If this strategy works for you, that's great. However, I do know that there's a new remnant of Scribes arising that's ready to ditch the scripts and implement heaven's blueprint to their businesses as they partner with God. When you aren't clear on the people that are drawn to you or the message that resonates with them, you will experience a disconnect when you're writing. You will know their 'why' when you ask and have an honest conversation. Building your audience and engaging with your community as you write the book is a great idea.

I will now address two focus pillars which are: a) Attracting the right people who are assigned to you with your voice and b) letting go of people who can't go with you into your next season.

a. You will only know who resonates with your message when you show up consistently on your social media platform if you're doing organic marketing (e.g. going live once a week speaking on key concepts of your upcoming or published book in your community). When you speak, you release a sound in the atmosphere that either pulls someone in or repels them. Storytelling is a gifted tool that paints a picture of your authenticity. People are drawn to vulnerability because they don't have to pretend to be someone they're not. As you evolve as a personal brand, your audience changes. When you fully express what you stand for and what you don't tolerate your 'tribe' will find you. Pay attention to the content your community engages with the most and create more of that. *Your oil is not for everyone. Discern who you pour into.* When we take off the blinders and flow within His rhythm, we stand a greater chance of uncluttering outdated strategies that keeps us boxed in. Trends are popular but not spiritual. It's not a one size fits all. Being a carbon copy of someone else will downplay your creativity and originality. Even the words, 'Speak your truth' used in online messaging was hijacked and misused for personal gain by Christian coaches. Before you make any statement or quote a doctrine, check the Source. Your perfect fit client will more than often share similar values and perceive you as a trusted voice they can glean from. You're not called to everyone and will have to sift out who you're not called to by asking relevant questions, so you don't compromise your Kingdom values.

b. Outgrowing people is inevitable. You may be ridiculed for making next level moves and leaving people behind, but they're God's responsibility, not yours. Be cautious not to make an idol of holding on to people the Lord told us to release. You can only take someone as far as they're willing to go. When following God's blueprint for your life it won't make sense to everyone. When you're surrounded by individuals who embrace comfortability your zealous goals will feel like intimidation because it reminds them of their stagnancy. You will begin to feel frustrated when your vision seems far-fetched to leaders who don't have the capacity or the character to meet you where you are and about to go. This also pertains to shifting your audience and leaving groups that's not anointed to pour into you. Your spiritual appetite changes when you get off the milk to make room for substance and in-depth learning so you can apply as you give an account of your inspirational story. When you are connected to the right destiny helpers it will serve as a catalyst for your building season. A tree can only bear fruit when its leaves are pruned. As the Lord chastises us, He will cut away desires of the flesh so that we can get rid of attitudes and behaviors that don't honor Him. Your fruit will testify of the goodness of God.

Your relationships will undergo a pruning process where the separation will be an indication of who should get access to you. Stewarding your resources and time well during this transition will be the determining factor as you re-introduce yourself to your 'tribe'. I use the word tribe loosely so you can identify with individuals who share similar beliefs and Christian values as you. To give an example, if your highest value is integrity, there will be an expectation that those you align with honors their word too. You'll be drawn to them instinctively as you find common ground. You could also connect with someone's spirit and discern their motives before ever having a conversation. I believe there are people that carry the same spiritual DNA as you. Mary was Elizabeth's destiny helper in *Luke 1:41* and was on assignment to release a message to her that would change the trajectory of her life. John the Baptist leaped in Elizabeth's stomach after hearing Mary's voice and encountered Holy Spirit. That's the power that resides in us. When you use your voice, you influence atmospheres, but you must be associated with the right people. If their faith doesn't match yours then you're run the risk of aborting the mission He gave you.

While writing my third book, *Just Say No: 14 Transformational Keys to Set Healthy Boundaries in Business and Relationships* two years ago, that's exactly the areas I found myself challenged in which resulted in being more deliberate in communicating healthy boundaries in a personal and professional capacity. It preserves relationships and protects your peace. As prophetic visionaries we live the message before releasing it to the world, which is one of the distinct characteristics of a Scribe. That book is still transforming the lives of individuals who desire to overcome people-pleasing so they can be unimpeded in walking out their God-given assignments. Again, it was written in obedience after my husband, who is my accountability partner, prophesied that more books will be birthed and eventually I will start offering premium publishing services too. Of course, I downplayed my ability to pursue publishing, but His will is greater than ours.

Simply put, a Scribe communicates the heart of God through revelatory words and serves as His mouthpiece in their sphere of influence. This anointing transcends beyond flowing in writing into administrative gifts, creativity expressed through art and prophetic journaling. Were there Scribes in the Bible? Absolutely. They were influential writers who interpreted God's law and trained to write and record court proceedings. Their role was also to record historical events and interpret scripture.

Ezra was a Scribe. In Ezra 7:6 it asserts, *'this Ezra went up from Babylon. He was a scribe skilled in the Law (the five books) of Moses, which the Lord God of Israel had given; and the king granted him everything that he asked, for the hand of the Lord his God was on him.'*

Baruch was a Scribe. *"In the fourth year of Jehoiakim the son of Josiah, king of Judah, this word came to Jeremiah from the Lord, saying, "Take a* *scroll [of parchment] and write on it all the words which I have spoken to you concerning Israel and Judah, and all the nations, from the day I [first] spoke to you in the days of [King] Josiah until this day.*

Then Jeremiah called Baruch the son of Neriah, and Baruch wrote on the scroll of the book all the words which Jeremiah dictated, [words] which the Lord had spoken to him. Jeremiah commanded Baruch, saying, "I am [in hiding, virtually] restrained; I cannot go into the house of the Lord. So you go to the Lord's house on a day of fasting and read from the scroll the words of the Lord to the people which you have written as I dictated.

Then Baruch read to all the people the words of Jeremiah from the scroll of the book in the house of the Lord, in the chamber of Gemariah the son of Shaphan the scribe, in the upper court, at the entry of the New Gate of the Lord's house." (Jeremiah 36: 1-2, 4-5, 10)

Now that you have some idea of what an ancient Scribe's role was, I want to share some prophetic revelation on how it relates to modern-day Scribes in the marketplace. My goal is not to replace the biblical meaning of what a Scribe is, but to unlock the gift of writing in you and to ask the Lord how He wants you to apply it to your daily life. I always encourage personal revelations as you partner with Holy Spirit.

If you're a marketing strategist, you can tap into your creativity and spiritual gifts in the marketplace when crafting messaging for your clients. If you're a five-fold leader who stewards a coaching business, you can write with power from a position of spiritual authority and finish your book in an accelerated time because you're following His voice as to what topics and storyline to cover. If you're a content creator, you can repurpose your content and invite your community on a transformative journey with you as you receive heavenly downloads. If you're a purpose-driven mom raising children of destiny, you can creatively write a children's book to illustrate the love of God based on your personal experiences. I have so many ideas and I believe God has given me the ability to empower and prophetically guide my clients to craft the vision for their books and execute it in accelerated time by flowing in their gift as a Scribe. I have learned that not every vision is for now and was given to you to launch at an appointed time. I've experienced this first-hand when I felt led to pause projects to finish what I've started. I shifted my mindset from losing out to being aligned to His kairos time. We gain wisdom when taking a deeper look at failures and life lessons over the years. What we do with them is up to us. When you fully walk in your authenticity and anointing, you have an opportunity to unlock the Scribe in you. What qualifies you? Being available to be used by Him and giving your YES wholeheartedly.

Blending in is not your portion. Take it from me. Being overlooked in my twenties and thirties was a blessing. We were created with a sense of belonging innately inside of us that only God can fill. When you seek validation from others you will be disappointed. *Be encouraged that when you find yourself, your tribe will be attracted to you.* When you pretend to be someone else it will burn you out and be rooted in falsehood. As you step into your authenticity, you may be tempted to go back to your old ways of doing things. Bury it. He has a new garment for you. The reason why you were refused a seat at the table of those you admired is because you were destined to have your own. Not every stage is for you. You need to protect the gift He has deposited in you. He is giving you the platform to write so you can influence lives throughout the globe with your story.

Build the community you desire to be a part of, so that you don't have to feel the urge to fit into rooms that weren't designed for you. I joined a coaching program last year that sounded good with all the bells and whistles. I resonated with the name and the outcomes it was promising in the marketing message. A few months into the program something felt off. They were big on 'culture' and not spamming members in the group. But that wasn't the issue. I started praying about my participation and the Lord started to reveal red flags to me. Manipulation was used as a tool to lure me in. God never instructed me to be part of the community because we don't share similar values and are unequally yoked. I repented. He exposed me to it, so you don't have to repeat the same mistakes I made. This lesson served a purpose. Seek Him first before you enter any business covenants.

I launched my community, **The Wealthy Kingdom Authors Academy**, in 2022 so that Scribes have a creative space to fully express who they are as they write their stories. That same year I received the words, 'Wealth Alignment' from the Lord that I used as the foundational pillar of the online academy as we cultivate movements to finance Kingdom missions. Again, if the community you've been praying for doesn't exist, create it. Pioneers build differently. I also believe that if someone in your industry provides a similar service, you don't have to feel intimidated, because no-one can copy your originality. It's your obedience to execute the idea that matters. I interviewed a prophetic Scribe on one of my tv show episodes and she made a powerful statement that I'll never forget. She said the Lord instructed her to write her book in 90 days or the window of opportunity would close. Wow. Imagine not fulfilling your assignment and someone else being chosen to give birth to what He originally gave you. *Think about that.* You can only produce fruit when you decide to stay committed to the prophetic vision for your book, whatever it takes. How disciplined are you to steward a personal brand that honors God? The tables He will seat you at in this season is to blaze a trail for the next generation. People are drawn to you because you're different as you lead with biblical principles. *You belong to a royal priesthood.*

When you're invited as a speaker to local book clubs, corporate conferences, and international virtual stages, your book will give you the credibility to be seen as an expert in your field. Your gift is about to make room for you. Do you believe that? He is elevating the underdog into a position of authority as His mouthpiece. He chose you for a time such as this.

In the next chapter we will break down Kingdom concepts that will give you the confidence to say YES to your God-calling and function as a prophetic Scribe so that you can amplify your authority in the marketplace.

JOURNAL PROMPT: Take 10-15 minutes in your day to prophetically prayer journal and talk to the Lord. You can read the word and play soft worship music in the background if you feel led to do so. Ask the Lord which environment, friendship, or group you should no longer be a part of that's hindering you from fulfilling your purpose. Pray for wisdom and destiny helpers. Record the date and year that you've asked the question so that you can go back to it when the Lord answers your prayer.

WORD OF ENCOURAGEMENT

"When you mind His business, He takes care of your business."
~Dr. Megan Bruiners

CHAPTER FOUR

Clarity on your assignment

Before pursuing coaching in the year 2020 when a global pandemic brought the entire world to a complete standstill, I had a successful flying career as a flight attendant for fourteen years. In the same year I stepped into the prophetic call of God on my life. I will be using my story to highlight some paradigm shifts that were catalysts in catapulting me into getting clarity on my next assignment. I transitioned from having an employee mindset while working in a job to being deployed as a Kingdom entrepreneur and partnering with God in my business. My value was determined by an employer who paid me a monthly salary based on what he deemed I deserved for the number of hours I sacrificed being away from my family. It was only a pitstop and my training ground that prepared me to speak into the lives of thousands of pioneers across the globe. I experienced many layovers in Ghana, London, New York, Washington DC, Australia, Hong Kong, Munich, Frankfurt, Sao Paulo, Maldives, and many other countries that will leave lasting memories for the next generation. Two years leading up to my retrenchment I received a vision from God that my time was slowly coming to an end. I released control of how my next assignment was supposed to unfold and embarked on a journey I haven't looked back on since then. As a first-generation entrepreneur there was no blueprint on how to steward an online business and build a personal brand. My acceleration as an author four years ago was attributed to following His directions and seeing it as a calling, not a job.

Have you seen any similarities in your own story? Perhaps, you were in a corporate job, and He called you to start your own consultancy firm having years of expertise. If you're currently employed full-time and desire to start a business, then understanding your assignment will give you an advantage. You may even be in retirement with purpose flowing through your veins and a new vigor to chase your dreams so that you can leave a legacy for your grandchildren. *Go for it. I'm rooting for you!* We need your words of wisdom. Where you find yourself now is only for a season, and you're only passing through. He is showing you what's possible when you trust Him wholeheartedly.

It took me four years to embody seeing myself as a thought leader. It started with unlearning false beliefs about myself and renewing my mind before my outward behavior could change. Thought leadership is when you've mastered your message and made it your own without borrowing someone else's quotes. It's your intellectual property. You create your own taglines. You write your own scripts. Imagine what you can accomplish tapping into unlocked potential and co-creating with God. Many leaders have settled with what life has thrown at them without questioning why they were in the wilderness to begin with. When you don't have clarity on your assignment, then you're going to give your time to anyone who demands it. Your brand message is attached to you knowing what you're supposed to do on the earth opposed to keeping busy and merely existing. If you're going to finish your book as a Scribe you will have to learn to say NO. You can't afford to be connected to people who lack vision for their own life. It may sound harsh, but it's a reality that you'll have to face. I've seen many leaders abort their assignment of writing their story because of the fear of man and being judged for exposing secret sin. When you truly believe that what you've overcome was to set someone else free, your convictions will be greater than your fear.

Our seasonal assignments are a series of tasks that eventually lead us to our calling. Your uncompromising YES activates the seed that was dormant in you for all the years. If we want to live in the promises of God, there is a responsibility to act on what we've heard through prayer. Every step of obedience takes us closer to fulfilling our purpose. Confusion creeps in when you're misaligned with your assignment and season. That's the reason your circle matters. You can be busy with ten projects and still miss Him if it's not what you're purposed to do over that specific time frame. When you feel overwhelmed by the demands of life it's best to become still and to listen before making your next move. Spend time with God and ask Him if you're still on track. When you are presented with new opportunities you will intuitively know what to do because you've soaked in His presence. *Is what you are prioritizing now moving the needle for you in life and business?*

Cookie-cutter frameworks

Comparison delays us from stepping into the fullness of our prophetic destinies. It's a huge distraction and steals our joy. If you're going to amplify your voice on global platforms, there's no room for doubt. You will grieve your old self as you shed off layers of who you used to be. You're going through a metamorphosis. When you find yourself at this threshold of new beginnings, you will have an impulse to go back to familiarity. You no longer reside at that address. You'll be tempted to jump on the bandwagon of what's trending in the online space. I implore you to take the time to work through the first few chapters while meditating on relevant scriptures so that you know whose you are, and it's embedded in you. As a Scribe you will face internal battles as you steward the message He has given you. The good news is that you don't have to feel pressured to be a carbon-copy of gifted leaders in your sphere of influence. That's what makes you unique.

As the curator of three International Multi-Author collaborative book projects, every assignment was different. I received the vision for the book cover, the theme, featured authors, package tiers, the marketing strategy, and finer details in my business meeting with God. Prior to launching my own collaborative book series, I was a co-author in another book project, *Ambitious Women Rise*, which inspired me to be the visionary of my own so I could empower countless leaders to make an impact in their communities. Anthologies are now gaining popularity, and more stories are being unleashed to transform lives. I remember asking the Lord if leading these book projects was still something He wanted me to pursue or if it was seasonal. Let's just say He instructed me to stay on the wall and keep on building. When you don't have clarity on your assignment, you'll put your tools down when you should be planning for what's next. You won't feel compelled to give things away for free when you should be charging premium prices. If you desire to steward an author business, you need to be clear on your pricing structure when compiling short stories of leaders in your community. If it's a passion project and you have sponsorships to fund it, go all in. If it forms part of your business model, it's important to do a cost analysis before starting, lest you lose profits when facilitating them. It should make financial sense as a business owner offering an all-inclusive service. I will expand on this strategy on how to grow your personal brand as a Kingdom Author in chapter seven. Ask the Lord for a strategy on how He wants you to steward your solo or co-authored book projects even if it has never been done before. I'm speaking to my eagles right now who are called to impact lives and be the first domino.

Soaring with the eagles

Eagles have accurate vision regardless of the obstacles ahead of them. You're built to soar with the eagles and to be courageous. That's why you were drawn to the message in this book. When you're intentional to connect the dots of your life story, you'll see the signs were there all along. You have the determination to succeed. As a leader you've endured many hardships and experienced great losses but by the grace of God you got back up again. Getting into rooms with like-minded leaders will be the game-changer for you as a Scribe who values personal development. Narrow-minded people will always find a way to bring you down because of the light in you. Your wilderness experience is only your passage to get to the other side so that you can testify about all the Lord has done. Some leaders park there and get infected by 'wilderness thinking syndrome' which becomes the foundation of their decisions. *Not you.* You were only passing through and had no intention of going around the same mountain. *Again. And again.* You were assigned to disrupt the status quo.

In Isaiah 40: 31 (AMP) it states, *'But those who wait for the Lord [who expect, look for, and hope in Him] Will gain new strength and renew their power; They will lift up their wings [and rise up close to God] like eagles [rising toward the sun]; They will run and not become weary, They will walk and not grow tired.'*

Whatever season you're finding yourself in, this too shall pass. At an appointed time, He will clothe you with supernatural strength, favor, and a peace that surpasses all understanding that even your enemies will be astounded. Sometimes it's those closest to you that betray your trust, but He already provided a way for you to manage the pain. He was protecting you. Eagles use the storm to fly to greater heights smaller birds hide from and rise above life's challenges. My prayer is that your spiritual sight will be restored so that you can prophesy to areas of barrenness, lack of vision, and to hear His voice clearly so that you can birth the book He anointed you to write. If you're a prophetic person that is gifted to receive revelation through dreams and visions, you can access the spiritual realm as a Scribe to unlock new dimensions with guidance from Holy Spirit.

When I transitioned from being a follower to a leader it took courage because I avoided confrontation and raising my opinion in personal and business relationships for the first thirty years of my life. Imagine being riddled with fear of what you're going to say and how it will be received. Leadership taught me that humility and vulnerability are necessary characteristics to have. The Lord pushed me out of my comfort zone and gave me the tenacity to break free from my insecurities and the fear of failure. You already know that He gives you authority where you feel the most inadequate. My confidence grew with every step of faith and my creativity increased which led me to prophetically see the vision for the books He called me to write to empower my clients. *I surrendered my way of doing it.* Did I make mistakes? Loads of them. But I kept at it and stayed consistent. I was thinking about the seasoned ministry leader who is still healing from church hurt with a powerful message of forgiveness. I'm showing up for the global visionary who has lost a loved one and is in a season of grieving because it awakened parts of her childhood memories. It was for the high-level consultant who had an absent father and experienced trauma most of her upbringing because of disappointment. If you led a life of any kind of addiction, there are many lives dependent on your testimony because that was part of my story too. You are not defined by your past mistakes. *You are more than overcomers. Your voice matters.*

While I was processing significant events that happened leading up to speaking on virtual stages as an entrepreneur, I used the highs and lows as story points when presenting. As you embark on this journey as a Kingdom author, I would encourage you to write down defining moments that impacted you to shift your perspective. It will serve as a great resource for you so you can have content on the go. You can create a storyboard or journal for reference when outlining your chapters or key points for your message as a keynote speaker. You'll be able to plan your content months in advance without feeling overwhelmed, and use pertinent stories for your book. Flowing in your zone of genius will set you apart in your industry. It's not God's plan for your life to be the best kept secret. I trust you're all fired up to embrace your story with all its imperfections.

In the next chapter we are activating your spiritual gifts so you can partner with Holy Spirit in your writing. You'll also discover the blueprint of merging your faith with your business as a Scribe. Posture your heart to receive fresh insight, knowledge, and understanding as you trust Him to reveal the primary gifts you're flowing in. If this concept is new to you, be assured that every good and perfect gift comes from above (James 1:17).

JOURNAL PROMPT: Take 5-10 minutes to prophetically prayer journal and talk to the Lord. You can read the word and play soft worship music in the background if you feel led to do so. Ask Him to reveal to you any significant events in your life that can be used as part of your testimony. Keep those notes in a safe place after you've recorded the year and date in your journal.

SCRIPTURE FOR REFLECTION

"Now there are distinctive varieties and distributions of endowments (gifts, extraordinary powers distinguishing certain Christians, due to the power of divine grace operating in their souls by the Holy Spirit) and they vary, but the [Holy] Spirit remains the same."
~1 Corinthians 12:4

Part Two

CHAPTER FIVE

Flowing in your gifts

The Lord revealed to me that as Kingdom leaders we have separated flowing in our gifts from our roles as coaches, consultants, authors, and speakers transforming lives in the marketplace. Being a Scribe is only a facet of you being who God called you to be. *It's one prophetic expression.* When you see writing as an interruption to your busy schedule it will just be another task to complete. As you articulate yourself when you're speaking, you authentically give language to your story by writing it down and effortlessly use your voice to draw in your reader. It shouldn't be different to what you're already mastering. What starts out as a seed eventually bears fruit when watered, nurtured, and cultivated. Your confidence needs to grow in your journey of becoming. If you're a kindergarten teacher your level of patience is much higher than someone who is not skilled in the industry. When you design a children's book you have the knowledge and insight to recognize what would be themes that can be used for illustration. You can be talented in what you do but when you flow in your gift, He gives you the divine ability to tap into the supernatural. As a vessel of God in the marketplace you were chosen to represent Him. When you're an influencer and ambassador for Jesus Christ your personal brand will have a different standard. It's your marketplace ministry outside of the four walls of the church. When you merge your faith with your book business.

As a marketplace and ministry leader it was not always easy to show up functioning effortlessly in both roles. Again, there was no blueprint to follow other than the traditional route. As a book consultant and Scribe the primary gifts that I tap into when writing are exhortation, prophetic, and gift of faith. It's not who I am, but what I do. I adapt depending on the platform that I'm on. Whether it's a virtual boardroom or ministry camp, the foundation is built on prayer. The only difference between the two is that in business my premium services come at a cost, and we don't blur the lines by communicating it's a free service. Our callings are unique and assigned to us by our Heavenly Father. In one season you'll be employed in a corporate job while working part-time in your business after hours. In another, you could be serving in full-time ministry and trusting the Lord for a consistent income so you can finance the vision He gave you. For years I believed that if ministry wasn't preaching behind the pulpit every Sunday it was wrong. I was detoxing from religion. As my ministry grew it inspired me to write my fifth book, *Unlock Your Voice, Vol. II: Mantles, Mandates and Motherhood* that reached bestseller status on Amazon and featured five co-authors.

You may be thinking how flowing in your gifts relates to you writing a book. It forms an intricate part of your untold story. It's how I finished my manuscript in less than thirty days without procrastinating. It's how you will courageously publish your book in 90 days when you implement the steps throughout this book.

I've encountered many anointed women leaders who felt that their busy schedule should be empty before they started with their outline when discipline and prioritizing were the missing pieces. Imagine how many impactful stories would be released into the world to advance the Kingdom of God if visionaries fully operated in their gifts. When you have the winning formula, you'll be able to finish your chapters written in an accelerated time without worrying about writer's block. To give you an example, I created the outline for this book in less than one hour. The revelation you receive from co-authoring with Holy Spirit is unmatched when it's combined with learning a new skill and embracing your talent. *That's your superpower so you can be bold and courageous.* Distractions will *take you off the path you're supposed to go so you take longer to get the results you planned for. Let's address possible hindrances to flowing in your God-given assignment and spiritual endowments.*

1. Too much noise

The only voice you should be attuned to is that of Holy Spirit if you desire to be laser-focused in prioritizing your highest values. When you allow anyone to pour into you there is a risk that they have wrong intentions and are praying against you. Not all voices are pure prophetic voices. When you know that the Lord instructed you to spend more time taking care of your emotional-being first and a coach/counselor advises you to keep on pushing the sales in your business regardless of how you feel, that's a red flag. This is one of the reasons so many entrepreneurs get stagnant and confused about their next move. Our actions should be aligned with what we have heard in the secret place when no-one was watching no matter how convincing the noises of friends, family, and business relationships are. Not everything that is good is inspired by God.

2. Unwillingness to receive

Everyone loves giving, but only a few are open to receiving from others. Your destiny helper may be near you, but you've put up a fence because your trust was broken in past relationships. As a result, you're not fully invested in programs and start tasks but don't finish them. We've all been there. When you pray for divine mentorships or assistance it will not present itself the way you envisioned it to be. The person assigned to you could be in another country from a completely different background with a genuine heart to serve God and His people. Don't miss out on what God has for you and be open to receive His blessings before rejecting help from others. We're not designed to build on our own in the Kingdom of God.

3. Overthinking the process

If at this stage you're still unclear about the message for your book, you can pause and think about your own story and what you've overcome. *Keep it simple.* What can you talk about for hours without it feeling like a chore. He is also healing you while you're writing so give yourself grace. With every step of faith you take He is revealing the ultimate blueprint for your life. Come out of agreement with doubt, unbelief, and procrastination as you surrender your uncertainty to Him. You're uncluttering and getting rid of old thinking patterns. Do a prophetic act and clear out your closet by removing old clothes. Let go of old habits by speaking out loudly about what you're not settling for anymore. Change your perspective from being anxious about lack of finances to using the resources you have in your hand which is invaluable.

4. Don't chase six-figures, seek Him for strategy first

When you follow your purpose, money will follow you. Check your Source if you're on a journey of discovery so you're not pulled onto platforms you're not quite ready for. Discern those opportunities that promise a quick fix while hustling your way through. When you stay within His purposeful rhythm it eventually leads you into the rooms you've been predestined to be. When you execute the assignment He has given you, the five and six figure corporate contracts will find you in His appointed time.

5. Set boundaries and delegate mundane tasks

Time is a resource and should be managed well. Being purpose-driven is one of the ways in which I get things done. The enemy's agenda is to steal your time, so you don't accomplish the Kingdom mission God set out for you which opens the door to your next. If you're an entrepreneur, start building your dream team by outsourcing individuals who are skilled and gifted in a particular function so that you can delegate tasks in your business and free up some of your time. When stewarding a personal brand, you will need a basic marketing funnel to lead your community to your books and resources as you expand your reach.

Say YES to the mantle on your life

Let's look at Jonah, (the only prophet to attempt to abandon his divinely appointed mission) ran from the call on his life *in Jonah 1: 10-17, "Then the men became extremely frightened and said to him, "How could you do this?" For the men knew that he was running from the presence of the Lord, because he had told them. Then they said to him, "What should we do to you, so that the sea will become calm for us?"—for the sea was becoming more and more violent. Jonah said to them, "Pick me up and throw me into the sea. Then the sea will become calm for you, for I know that it is because of me that this great storm has come upon you." Nevertheless, the men rowed hard [breaking through the waves] to return to land, but they could not, because the sea became even more violent [surging higher] against them. Then they called on the Lord and said, "Please, O Lord, do not let us perish because of taking this man's life, and do not make us accountable for innocent blood; for You, O Lord, have done as You pleased." So they picked up Jonah and threw him into the sea, and the sea stopped its raging. Then the men greatly feared the Lord, and they offered a sacrifice to the Lord and made vows. Now the Lord had prepared (appointed, destined) a great fish to swallow Jonah. And Jonah was in the stomach of the fish three days and three nights."*

If you're a prophetic person I'm sure you can relate to Jonah's story, and maybe finding yourself in the exact same position. I found myself running from the call back and gave my YES alongside my husband back in 2019. The significance of this date was that this same year my father lost his battle to stage four stomach cancer a few months after attending my pastoral ordination. I don't believe this was a coincidence as I've been prayer journaling for years for my father's salvation. God orchestrated it so he could witness me stepping into my calling and then being led to the Lord by my husband one month before he took his last breath. I wrote my book shortly afterwards which was inspired by my grief journey and being awakened to purpose after a great loss in my family. Every small step of obedience leads to our prayers being answered.

What will it cost you to embrace your mantle? Who have you given your authority away to?

Your relationships will shift when you stop downplaying your gifts and say no to things not in alignment with your assignment. People will leave and cut you off without an explanation. This is not a reflection of you, but an indication that you've outgrown them and want more out of life. *There is power in a made-up mind.* Separating from unfruitful relationships is part of the refining process. As you navigate through the pain of leaving others behind, think about how Abraham must have felt when God instructed him to leave everything behind to follow Him. He went as far as sacrificing his son of the promise, Isaac, to stay in the will of God. When you start getting more visible in your community and master your message with confidence, you will attract destiny killers. Prepare your heart for disappointment because not everyone will understand your vision or the blueprints He has given you. The purging of personal and business relationships will shape your character as you withstand the resistance of breaking through to the other side. Whatever decision you take, you won't please everyone. We were not designed to manage people's emotions, only our own. God desires for you to be whole: mind, soul, body, and spirit. If your healing is compromised, then you may have settled for living below your maximum potential. If you're honest with yourself, what's the reason you have been avoiding becoming visible as a coach, speaker, creative leader, or Kingdom author. Name the underlying fear that could be masquerading as being overly cautious because you find it difficult to trust anyone. Manage any unrealistic expectations so you're not seeking approval from others.

Just like Jonah, when we're not in the place we're supposed to be, every individual connected to us will be affected by our disobedience. *That's huge.* Imagine being in the stomach of a fish for three days and three nights. Whew. This is why writing your book in His kairos time as a Scribe elevates you into rooms you're not 'qualified' to speak in, but the Lord's plan prevails because He wants you to enlarge your territory for His glory. Remember, the window of opportunity will not be for a lifetime. It will save you many years to just BE who He created you to be, unapologetically.

Birth the mission. Start the movement. Leave the outcomes to God.

Amplifying your Authority

In *Genesis 1:28* God commanded Adam and Eve to be fruitful, multiply, and to fill the earth and subdue it. This Kingdom principle is our anchor for establishing our authority in the marketplace, however, our faith will be put to the test. You can be a go-to expert in your industry and still void of mastering areas in your life which shows up as inconsistencies. *When you experience pressure from all sides, do you pursue the things of God and press through, or do you allow emotions to dictate your future? When you clearly heard His voice to write the book, did you work through the pain of your story, or did you avoid it? If you've been hurt by the church, did you blame God for what people did to you or did you pray for unforgiveness in your heart?*

We can only be fruitful when we embrace the truth of God's word and navigate through the hard seasons because this is the place where our spiritual muscles are exercised. To occupy the promised land, we need to make peace with the process to get there. You can write twenty bestseller books and be considered to be in the top 1% authority in your sphere of influence while having no power, because you are solely focused on the accolades and not your spiritual well-being. When you're purpose-driven then your motives are not only driven by accomplishments, but how well you are managing your seed so that it can multiply. He can only cultivate what we are prepared to grow which will require us to demolish cracked foundations so that we can break any patterns that would fuel us to withdraw every time we have to make a big decision. Amplifying your authority is two-fold which speaks to the influence you have as a faith-based entrepreneur and the other is the weight of your assignment in relation to the mandate He has given you. I believe the reason leaders are not walking in dominion is because their spiritual authority has been taken away from them so that they're exempted from experiencing His resurrected power in their business, ministry, and personal life. In the natural this can look like muted voices, compromise, passivity, dysfunctional patterns, toxic relationships, identity crisis, and barrenness which has a root cause. When these are not dealt with, it shows up when we're stewarding our businesses and the resources He has given us. With having a multitude of prophetic voices fighting for your ear in this era, being self-led when it comes to seeking God for yourself concerning your next season and external shifts is key. The more you move past the discomfort, the more diligent you become in navigating new territories because you're not overthinking your next steps. You're totally dependent on Him to give you directions. When we are placed into a position of authority our fruit speaks volumes.

Accountability for your next level

I would not be a great destiny helper if I missed the opportunity to speak to you about the importance of accountability as you create generational wealth in the marketplace as a Scribe.

In Deuteronomy 8:18 it states: *'But you shall remember [with profound respect] the Lord your God, for it is He who is giving you power to make wealth, that He may confirm His covenant which He swore (solemnly promised) to your fathers, as it is this day.'*

We have been given the ability to function in our spiritual gifts and generate Kingdom wealth so we can fund Faith-driven missions. You don't have to choose. Stewarding your finances well is a game changer. Who keeps you on track? Someone that can bring you back into alignment when you find yourself at a crossroad in life. When God removes any hindrances to your purpose it would be beneficial to pray for a trusted circle to share your dreams with. Jesus walked with the twelve disciples, but only had three in close proximity to Him while accomplishing the will of the Father on this earth. While you're asking the Lord who these individuals are in your life you can totally depend on Holy Spirit to be your intercessor and counselor. A person can never take His role. However, who you are associated with in this season will be the determining factor for you fulfilling your mandate. Someone that identifies your blind spots and corrects you when you're not stewarding your resources well. They've been where you are planning to go.

While writing this book I reached out to one of my mentors for accountability because there is power in agreement. It empowered me to keep track of my progress, so I'm set to reach all my timelines. It's a Kingdom principle as you stretch your faith and allow God to do a supernatural work through you. I also want to remind you that you're not alone. There are genuinely individuals that are anointed to walk with you. It may just be that you haven't found them yet. I want you to win and take hold of everything the Lord has for you. *It's your birthright.* If you must unlearn old methods, do that. It takes a village to build a personal brand, and He is training you to accept divine assistance. No begging. Just receiving what He wants to give to you. In *Genesis 1:28* God commanded Adam and Eve **to be fruitful**, **multiply**, and to fill the earth and **subdue it.** This Kingdom principle is our anchor for establishing our authority in the marketplace, however, our faith will be put to the test. You can be a go-to expert in your industry and still void of mastering areas in your life which shows up as inconsistencies. *When you experience pressure from all sides, do you pursue the things of God and press through, or do you allow emotions to dictate your future? When you clearly heard His voice to write the book, do you work through the pain of your story, or do you avoid it? If you've been hurt by the church, do you blame God for what people have done to you or pray for unforgiveness in your heart?*

We can only be fruitful when we embrace the truth of God's word and navigate through the hard seasons because this is the place where our spiritual muscles are exercised. To occupy the promised land, we need to make peace with the process to get there. You can write twenty Bestseller books and be considered to be in the top 1% authority in your sphere of influence while having no power because you are solely focused on the accolades and not your spiritual well-being. When you're purpose-driven then your motives are not only driven by accomplishments, but how well you are managing your seed so that it can multiply. He can only cultivate what we are prepared to grow which will require us to demolish cracked foundations so that we can break any patterns that would fuel us to withdraw every time we have to make a big decision.

Amplifying your authority is two-fold which speaks to the influence you have as a Faith-based entrepreneur and the other is the weight of your assignment in relation to the mandate He has given you. I believe the reason leaders are not walking in dominion is because their spiritual authority has been taken away from them so that they're exempted from experiencing His resurrected power in their business, ministry and personal life. In the natural this can look like voices that are being muted, compromise, passivity, dysfunctional patterns, toxic relationships, identity crisis and barrenness which has a root cause. When these are not dealt with, it shows up when we're stewarding our businesses and the resources He has given us. With having a multitude of prophetic voices fighting for your ear in this era, being self-led when it comes to seeking

God for yourself concerning your next season and external shifts are key. The more you move past the discomfort, the more diligent you become in navigating new territories because you're not overthinking your next steps. You're totally dependent on Him to give you directions. When we are placed into a position of authority our fruit speaks volumes.

I am rejoicing that you made it this far in the book as we've set the foundation for God's blueprint to launch your book in 90 days and steward a Kingdom author brand. In the next chapter you will get my proven step-by-step process of how I finished this book manuscript in less than 30 days. Are you ready?

JOURNAL PROMPT: Get in a quiet place and take 5-10 minutes to prophetically prayer journal and talk to the Lord. You can read the word and play soft worship music in the background if you feel led to do so. Ask Him which areas have you been avoiding in your life and if you're still in alignment with where He wants you to be. Keep those notes in a safe place after you've recorded the year and date in your journal.

SCRIPTURE FOR REFLECTION

"In all your ways know and acknowledge and recognize Him,
And He will make your paths straight and smooth
[removing obstacles that block your way]."
~Proverbs 3:6

The Signature Blueprint to launch your book in 90 days

The precursor for following my step-by-step method for outlining your book is to take time to implement the first five chapters prior to this one. As you release your past mistakes and step into your future-self it's imperative that you write from a victor's perspective after working through the negative mindset blocks and past pain triggers. If not, you will experience that it's more difficult to flow in your chapters and nail the story lines because the healing process needs to start first. Prophetic prayer journaling is your go-to tool to surrender what you think you should focus on in the book by asking relevant questions when spending time with God. If you desire a paid author mentorship community to grow in as you heal while writing through prophetic journaling, then you can learn more about how to join at **The Wealthy Kingdom Scribe Incubator.**

Step one: Prophetic vision for your book

As a Scribe you should write the vision down and make it plain. Don't skip this step because you want the quickest way to publish. It will save you time and money to envision the bigger picture and work your way back to the beginning. It will also serve as your greatest motivator when your emotions become overwhelming, and your time is not managed well. Getting started with a new book, especially if it's your first time, can be daunting when you're lacking strategy and a well-thought-through plan. *Well, that's not you.* You got this one in the bag. Firstly, invite Holy Spirit with you on this journey. I dedicate one day in the week to brainstorm book ideas after getting some inspiration for titles on Amazon in my genre in the Bestseller categories as a reference. If you're naturally a creative person you can write down 2-3 captivating titles and come back to them after a week to see if it still captures your attention. At the same time, you want to think about attracting your ideal reader with a subtitle detailing what the book is about and invest in a bespoke book cover. Keep this information in your notes so you can revisit them after the first draft of the manuscript is done. Whenever you get a fresh spurge of inspiration, I encourage you to spend time asking the Lord who your message is for and what problem you should be solving. See yourself as the sought-after thought leader your community is waiting to celebrate. Dream with God for a minute and forget about the resources you're lacking. Envision the individual reading your book. How does it make you feel? What are you sensing? If the book theme feels right to you then go for it. Whatever topic you go with, do it wholeheartedly. If you have twenty book titles with different messages, choose one core theme for the one book that is the most aligned with the season you're in and what He is using you to boldly speak about in your community. Literally, it's that simple. Don't overthink it. My vision is typed out and stored in different places electronically so it's visible and I can update it on the go. You can do whatever works best for you. As you get clarity on your book theme and put timelines in place, ensure your daily tasks line up with your next 30 day goal. Be disciplined in sticking to creating the one book idea so you can meet your deadline. Once you've established the look and feel for the cover design and shared it with your graphic designer, you can start planning towards outlining the framework of your book. You can decide if you want to design your book cover at the beginning stage or while it's in the editing phase.

Step two: Time Management

Honestly, I had all the excuses not to finish this book while raising two toddlers under two while running an online author business and serving in ministry. Perhaps you have more than three projects running in the background, and you've been feeling convicted to get it done. *Just start.* When you do the heart work in previous chapters, you'll slow down long enough to follow His divine blueprint for your life. Now that we're on the same page, I have a confession to make. I became laser focused and paused some of my projects to give birth to this baby. I committed four hours to writing every single day and believe it was only by His grace that I finished it in record time without feeling overwhelmed. *I cracked the code and I'm sharing my secrets with you, so you don't have to waste four years of your life figuring it out.*

You can allocate two-to-four-hour time blocks to one day with breaks in between so you can create new content and get clarity on which testimony to complement every chapter. How well you manage your time and what you say no to will determine your success and progress. Distractions will tempt you, however, stay the course. Keep in mind that as you get a revelation you will encounter times where you must release emotions no longer serving you. Avoidance and unwillingness to deal with our issues only delays our time. If you need inspiration, change your scenery or go for walks in your neighborhood so you can get fresh ideas. Always have a notebook with you to jot down God-given ideas or content you can use. Scribes are positioned daily to receive wisdom and new insight so they can be good stewards of the message God has given them. If you do fall behind and miss a few days, allocate thirty minutes to your day for writing until you make more time to flow for uninterrupted consecutive days. I discovered in my writing program that when authors have a gap of more than two weeks, they find it harder to become disciplined again and to get it done. If you work full-time, catch up after hours or early in the morning before going to work. Find your own rhythm. Communicate your boundaries in your household and let the family know that you have an assignment with a deadline to meet. If you're not getting the support you desire, be steadfast to execute what He's given you in obedience.

Step three: Prophetic prayer journaling

I received a personal revelation about prayer journaling in 2016 when I was seeking clarity for my personal development, business, and spiritual growth. When I look back, I see the miracle of how the Lord answered all my prayers after renewing my thinking and setting me free from unhealed soul wounds. This activity should not prioritize our time meditating on the word, however, when used together you can expect exponential growth as you steward motherhood, entrepreneurship, and ministry. I will break down a simple exercise to get started if you desire to hear God's voice for your business and book.

- Set 10-15 minutes aside to journal while spending time with Him.
- Get into a quiet place (you can play soft worship music in the background) and posture yourself to listen.
- Ask one question pertaining to the area you need clarity in and wait.
- You will get spontaneous thoughts which you can write down in your journal (a scripture, divine strategy, prophetic word, or an encouragement.)

- Capture the date and year of the journal entry on top and go back to it when your prayer is answered.

This prophetic activity can also be used to journal through your emotions and release old narratives that's keeping you in the comfort zone. When you embrace the process and take time to work through grief or past events with prophetic prayer journaling as a tool, you will be able to finish your book in less than thirty days. If you need professional counseling for trauma or deeply embedded soul wounds, I encourage you to get the necessary support. Don't rush this step. If you need more guidance on this exercise, you can schedule a 60-minute prophetic strategy call with me (refer to the link in the latter part of the book) to facilitate the session with you.

Step four: Outlining your chapters

The sobering truth about writing a book about your life story is that, without giving a solution to the challenge the ideal reader is facing, it's not sustainable. The longevity of the book will be short-lived, and your message will not have the reach you've been praying for as a Kingdom author. Before you start writing, ask yourself these three questions if you want to make impact with your devotional, journal, or non-fiction book:

1. *Who is the book written for (what group of people or individual is currently engaging with your content or attracted to your voice)?*
2. *What problem are you solving based on your research, interview-style questionnaires or polls in the form of written posts taken in your community (this will give you clarity on the book theme)?*
3. *After the book is launched, what do you intend to do with it (speaking, coaching program, workshop, grow your brand)?*

My personal time for outlining this book was less than an hour without artificial intelligence because I wanted to break it down the way I visualized it and make room for Holy Spirit too as I wrote in my authentic voice. With the title of the book fresh in my memory and being confident in my message, I used frequently asked questions from my community as well as challenges that most of the leaders in my online author academy needed guidance on, to formulate my chapter titles. To create a memorable theme, you should focus on one underlying message, so your ideal reader stays engaged. Once you've decided on the theme, work towards the flow of your subsequent chapters. You should have a skeleton framework with the number of chapters you would need. This could change so allow God to disrupt your flow even after it's all written out. Refine it as you go. *Now breathe.* Ask the Lord to show you your own unique blueprint so that the steps you're implementing are meaningful to you. Let's consider another creative way: If you're mastering your message and have taken the time to do research on your dream audience, you can convert the keywords they use when searching online for your chapter headings and expand on them in your content. If you understand your ideal reader's problem and can give a solution for it, you're ten steps ahead of an individual writing on a similar topic. If necessary, chapters should be restructured in the editing phase so you can focus on getting the content on paper.

The next step would be to create a story bank that you can implement into relevant chapters. You can use the 3-5 story points and make full sentences combined with your key lessons, so you don't run out of ideas. This is the part where you will be stretched to tap into your spiritual endowments as He unlocks the Scribe in you. You can fill out the chapters with strategies, personal experiences, testimonies, and lessons learned, depending on the type of book you plan on launching. If this is your first book it would be ideal if you used some of the stories you healed from while journaling if it aligns. Focus on getting one substantial chapter done and read it back to yourself so you can hear it in your authentic voice. Use your powerful story as your anchor to engage with your ideal reader. Repeat this same process for the remaining chapters. *How are you doing so far?*

Your first three chapters could speak to your breakdown, the middle chapters address your transformation, and the final chapters highlight your breakthrough moments for a non-fiction book. If you're a coach or consultant and want to create a handbook for leaders, you can use this leadership book to outline eight or ten principles based on your expertise. This is a go-to approach if you're not quite ready to release your personal testimony, but only certain elements of it that compliments the key concepts in the book. If you're repurposing content as an expert from speaking or podcasting, it's simply a matter of re-arranging the content you already have and making sure it's relevant to what your overall theme, personal story, and vision is. Whatever message you're conveying, show up as a thought leader and own your story. A leadership book is where you showcase your expertise and area of authority. A memoir or non-fiction book is your personal testimony, convictions, and overcomer story. Another example could be a compilation of short stories or poems. Choose a writing style that works best for you with the end-goal in mind. If you do need clarity on what content or story would be pertinent for the book you can journal through some ideas and seek direction from the Lord. If a painful memory presents itself, you will receive the wisdom to gracefully capture the words that would be the best fit for the topic you're writing on. Keeping a positive mindset is key so that you can manage your thoughts effectively when sudden feelings arise that make you question what others will say. Talk back to yourself and stand on who God says you are.

When you get to the body of your non-fiction book where you speak about your transformation, you need to let your ideal reader know what led you to being an authority and a voice to impact lives. Embody who you want to become and give your audience breakthrough strategies of how you are living out your message courageously from a place of victory. Give them the solutions they're looking for and show up confidently in your message. When you've made it pass this step, you're closer to the finish line so keep your momentum. If you need inspiration or a burst of energy do a fun activity in your break time. As a senior flight attendant during my layovers in Accra, on route to Washington DC on a 7-day trip, I glanced at the pool from my room on the third floor while finishing the chapters of my first book. While my colleagues frolicked in the water, I kept my eye on the prize. On another international flight I would rest or go for dinner and celebrate the small wins whenever I reached my goals. You would always find me with a pen and paper onboard my flights 36 000 feet above sea level because of the impartation I received from the Lord while traveling. I lost my usual rhythm of writing after having my children and had to adjust to my new lifestyle. The strategies that worked in a previous season were re-evaluated and I went with the pace of grace because I evolved. Frustration is a sign that He wants to give you a new blueprint so you can do it in a way that was never done before. When I slowed down and paused from the rat race, that's when I started seeing results and wrote my sixth book in less than thirty days.

When you feel stuck at a particular chapter, take regular breaks and deep breaths so you can orientate yourself again. You can revisit it again when your productivity and creativity flow again. Don't miss out on the inspiration right in front of you whether it's a random encouraging word from someone or spontaneous ideas flooding your mind. Get as much content out on paper once you're flowing and slot them into the relevant chapters as you complete the first draft of the manuscript. Your diligence is about to pay off so stay the course.

Step five: Finish first draft of manuscript

Once you've gained momentum you may feel led to expand on some paragraphs. If your manuscript is handwritten (this is by far the way to go) you can add detail to the storyline or include inspirational content. You can focus on the overall flow and detailing your chapters when typing it out. You will receive divine impartation and fresh insight as you release words creatively, so be prepared for any distractions so that you don't lose sight of the vision. It's advisable to read through the manuscript a few times and use Grammarly for minor grammar checks before investing in hiring a professional editor to review overall structure and quality while keeping your authentic voice. I would not recommend editing it on your own if you're building a personal brand. The editor will guide you on any missing pieces that's required after the first round. Everyone works differently so ask relevant questions before submitting your work so that there's no unnecessary delays. Think about asking 2-3 credible sources in your community to give you a review while it's in the editing phase or after it's been through the formatting process. You can use the endorsement for marketing purposes or include it in the publication of the book.

Step six: Editing & Formatting

The editing process can take 1-2 months depending on the word count and amount of work that is required. Some editors ask for a sample chapter and others request the number of words. There are different types of editing so it's important you do your research if it's not included in your publishing package, and you decide to self-publish. On some occasions the manuscript is formatted while being edited or after editing is being completed. During the formatting phase you will work alongside the publisher or formatter to work on the layout and design of your e-book and/or Paperback. You'll be able to give feedback and revise changes before it's ready for publishing. As a final quality check, it is recommended you do a final proofread of the manuscript before submitting it for publishing.

Step seven: Marketing campaign

Many authors skip this step and make the announcement for the book on their social media platforms a few days before it launches or even on the day. When executed correctly, this step can powerfully position you as a go-to-expert. When you position yourself as an authority it is recommended to promote the launch of your upcoming book long before it's published as part of a Bestseller strategy. When you take the first step of stewarding the vision, you can use it as an opportunity to engage in your community by writing posts or blogs covering some of the concepts you plan to cover. As a Kingdom author, marketing is the heartbeat of being a successful entrepreneur. If your publishing package includes a marketing plan, then it will save you time to plan it out yourself, especially if it's not your most favorite thing to do. If you're self-publishing it would be ideal to hire an expert with a proven method who specializes in the type of book you want to launch. You should also think about taking pre-orders before the book launches on Amazon or through your website, so that you can start getting some of your investment back. Another option is to have a launch team to build the excitement and release it on a set date while doing a countdown. The same principle can be followed for curating Multi-author collaborative book projects which increases your chances of becoming a Bestselling author. I will elaborate on this in chapter nine.

Step eight: Publishing

The success of this step depends on the publisher you choose to partner with if you're not self-publishing on an online platform. The latter is less expensive; however, it is worth investing in a professional publishing service if you want to launch a quality product and increase the credibility of your brand. You can make a profit from your book before publishing it when you partner with the right service provider who has a track record of successful clients who got results. If you're already blogging, podcasting, or contributing content on other people's platforms, you have an advantage. Think outside of the box if you desire to expand your reach and grow your network outside of your geographical location. If you decide to have a launch team you can communicate with them on how to spread the word of your book in a group setting, so everyone has access to the information and is ready for the launch day. The premium packages we curate include all of the above services so you as the author can get visible and focus on the marketing aspect pre-and post-launch day. You can schedule a 30-minute publishing consultation in the resource section of the book.

It takes a team to launch a successful marketing campaign and book that's geared towards amplifying your impact. If you're publishing on a huge platform like Amazon, it takes a few days to be approved, hence the launch date being a few days after hitting the publishing button. Ensure you order a proof copy to do a quality check of the Paperback before announcing the book is live. Get the support so that you can show up in your zone of brilliance. If you've considered going through a traditional publisher, you will not maintain creative control over the book process, your copyrights, or any profits per book sale. There is no guarantee that your manuscript will be approved, which is required to go through a literary agent and tedious process to qualify. When you self-publish or opt in to independently publish (you hire professionals to take care of the publishing process) you have full control of the creative process and the marketing of your book. You get higher royalty payouts with no limit on how many books you can publish on online self-publishing platforms.

Step nine: Launch Day

This is your moment to go all out. Throughout the day let your friends and family know that you just launched your book, and you would greatly appreciate their support. Have a checklist on standby so that you can cover everything you set out over those next three weeks and beyond. If you've assembled a launch team, then you would have ideally delegated admin tasks as you spread the word on all platforms. Your marketing efforts should increase at least seven days prior to launch and three weeks after leading up to your in-person or virtual book launch. Celebrate your wins as you amplify your authority in the marketplace.

Step ten: Post-launch

Marketing is not a once-off task as an author, but is a continuous activity. Expand your reach through global book distribution, being a guest on podcasts and radio interviews, media features, digital magazine features, scheduling Facebook lives discussing topics in the book with avid readers, chapter readings in small gatherings, intimate book club gatherings, five-week intensive book study, and local book tours.

This proven ten-step process, in combination with the pre-work and journal prompts, will position you to launch your book courageously in 90 days. If you need a community with accountability, then you can learn more about **The Wealthy Kingdom Scribe 90 Day Accelerator** when you follow the next steps at the end of the book. In the last few chapters, we will challenge you to think and dream bigger than what you see in your natural environment. Launching your book is only one aspect of you stewarding your message. Living it out courageously beyond the book launch is how you will be leaving your legacy for the next generation. The reality is that so many leaders have received a blueprint from God, but only a few execute it. When you fully step into your authority, anointing, and authenticity you will activate the seed inside of you so it can be multiplied. You can't pour from an empty cup and need a fresh revelation of who God says you are so that you can write from a place of rest and being filled by the Spirit of God. No more striving. Don't go back to the old way of doing it because He has a new garment for you. The old has gone and the new has come.

JOURNAL PROMPT: Get in a quiet place and take 5-10 minutes to prophetically prayer journal and talk to the Lord. You can read the word and play soft worship music in the background if you feel led to do so. Reflect on what stood out for you in previous chapters. Take your time to work through the emotions attached to your story that come up for you before moving onto the next part of this book. Ask the Lord to give you insight and understanding on how to apply the ten-step-process to your own life. Keep those notes in a safe place after you've recorded the year and date in your journal.

WORD OF ENCOURAGEMENT

"You were not called to be a carbon-copy of anyone else."
~Dr. Megan Bruiners

CHAPTER SEVEN

You are the Blueprint!

I almost burned my author business down following a million-dollar coach's blueprint for my brand. I will be sharing some of the key lessons from my personal experience so that you can spot the red flags in your own life. I wasn't seeking God in my decision to move forward, and trusted someone He never assigned to me in the first place. This individual was not my destiny helper. I began breaking down faulty foundations in my business model so that it reflected heaven's blueprint for my life. I ditched all formulas, scripts, frameworks, and templates that weren't honoring Him in my business. I repented and was committed to breaking it all down so it could be re-built again. Then the Lord gracefully stepped in, showed me the areas I wasn't stewarding well, and gave me His blueprint to build my personal brand. *When you've made peace with who you are to the core, you won't feel led to rebrand by changing your brand colors with every shift or re-write your titles in the marketplace because the work you do is rooted in your identity.* The transformation is taking place within you. You're evolving because you're the brand. We get a wake-up call whenever we're clinging onto resources instead of yielding to the instruction of the Source.

Promotion comes from God, and we should be in alignment with His plan and not be led by our emotions. You can be in the wrong place with people who don't have the authority to speak into your life based on your assignment and the season you're in. The plan of the enemy is to disarm you so that you can be distracted and fail to fulfill your prophetic destiny. Everything looks good from the outside, but there's a possibility that it's not a God thing, so discernment is key. Entrepreneurship will awaken unhealed trauma if it hasn't been dealt with. It's a continuous healing journey that builds stamina and character for the platform He called you to. In Chapter six, I listed my ten-step process so that you can courageously launch your book in 90 days. The transformation that happens while you write the book is going to empower you to live out your 'brand' message courageously. The great news is that you can always refer to those steps in whatever season you find yourself, while implementing the Kingdom principles throughout this book. *What behaviors or limiting beliefs can you identify with that's preventing you from fully embracing your call as a Scribe? Where have you watered down your message to fit into the expectations others have set out for you? Who are you without the title as a coach, pastor, or consultant?*

Living out your message courageously

If you're a purpose driven leader who desires to get into alignment with your calling through authorship, then your 'message' is connected to your story. I can't emphasize it enough that as you grow your message becomes refined depending on the audience you are speaking to. When you're in the boardroom you are creating strategies to market your 'brand' message which is the thing people will remember you by or how they perceive your personal brand before experiencing their transformation. If you're a first-time author that's still embracing thought leadership, you will get clarity about your personal message when you find your voice and have seen what's not working. It takes resilience to write your story, but it takes courage to live out your message and fully express who you are without being afraid of people projecting their opinions on you. Many authors have not quite lived out their unique message because it looks different to the status quo. You become disconnected from reality when you live your life for others or driven by producing twenty books for personal accomplishments without fulfilling your purpose. God searches our motives.

As you steward your author brand, you will encounter a series of small assignments as a Scribe because you are the blueprint! You're literally being tested and catapulted into your assignment before you can move into your next level. Your credibility as a thought leader starts with owning your story and confidence in using your voice to stand up for a cause beyond you. Understanding that you have influence in the domain He called you to will set you apart as a Kingdom author. Our wealth is connected to our obedience and through the currency of our ideas that we execute. You're an innovator and anointed to prosper in your business using Kingdom principles. There's more to wealth than finances which is only part of it. He is aligning you with people who are purpose pushers and have the resources that you need to finish your assignment. If you've been functioning in a role that you're not anointed or authorized to be in, there's an opportunity for you to take a detour and receive renewed vigor for your God-given calling. You may have felt convicted by Holy Spirit in one of your prophetic prayer journaling sessions while reflecting on your testimony and areas you desire breakthrough in. *Where have you crossed lanes with someone else's assignment you compared yourself with? Are you writing your book to prove a point to loved ones? Have you prayed for the person who your message is tailored to impact?*

These are some questions to ponder on that will disrupt any faulty thinking pattern that is hindering your progress. Many visionary leaders that believe in their message don't automatically live it out because it takes intentionality to stay consistent and show up authentically. Your community is drawn to you because of the obstacles you overcame and the greatness they see in you. You're an inspiration to people you've never met before, and you will do a disservice to them if you're not following through in launching your untold story. When you unfollow the old scripts, you will begin to unleash your own blueprints and experience change as you unlock the voices of the people you are called to. This is how you gain momentum in mastering your message and being seen as a go-to-expert in your field in the Kingdom of God. Mastery gets forged in the wilderness when you're in a cave season. It hits differently when you've been through everything you're writing about because it's based on experience and wisdom. Nobody can take your testimony away from you or describe the intricate details like you do. Courage is when you push past the fear, and you do it anyway. The tide is turning in your favor and you're about to see Him move on your behalf like never before. As you grow deeper in relationship with Him and seek truth, you will experience a true freedom to be yourself after years of pouring into someone else's vision. No more compromising your Kingdom values. Less convincing people to invest in your services. Your community should see you living out the standard you've set as a personal brand. In Luke 12:48 it reads, '*but the one who did not know it and did things worthy of a beating, will receive only a few [lashes]. From everyone to whom much has been given, much will be required; and to whom they entrusted much, of him they will ask all the more.*' If you need a good manager of your time and resources, He won't give you more because it will be mismanaged. *Can you be trusted with more?*

In another passage of scripture in Matthew 25:29 it states, "*For to everyone who has [and values his blessings and gifts from God, and has used them wisely], more will be given, and [he will be richly supplied so that] he will have an abundance; but from the one who does not have [because he has ignored or disregarded his blessings and gifts from God], even what he does have will be taken away.*"

Your workload will continue to pile up with a demand on your time increasing, leaving you feeling consumed. We can no longer use it as an excuse. If He gave you the desire to steward a Kingdom author brand, then the right people have been placed in positions to receive you as your name is being spoken in rooms you haven't heard of. *Whew.* He wants you to multiply the gift that was given to you and not sit on it. Go back to the original vision He showed you. *Are you ready to influence nations with your courageous story?*

Mindset of a Kingdom influencer

When you fully comprehend that the reason you went through the crushing seasons was to bring out the gold in you, you'll perceive your challenges through a different lens. It starts in the mind which is connected to our soul. It's when we've come to the realization that we're not what happened to us. You can live a fulfilled life when you separate what you do from who you are. Our relationships are a Kingdom currency and can set us back or propel us into destiny. You're not a victim of your circumstances because the battle has already been won. You have been given the victory. The giants in your life served a purpose so that you're totally dependent on God. In society there is a negative connotation to the word 'influencer' so I will give some insights on what it means considering the Kingdom. If you're a leader who is impacting lives, then you are influencing your community through your thoughts, actions, words spoken, and what you stand for. There is a responsibility to use the platform you've been entrusted with as an opportunity to take dominion and show up as an authority. *Not because of your works, but by faith.* When you give your power away to people because you feel inadequate to take up your royal position, you're indirectly saying that He didn't do a complete work within you. Having the mindset of a Kingdom influencer is built on the foundation of trusting God for your book, business, and ministry. One time while spending time with the Lord I received these words in my spirit, *'My people are not being visible because they've been taught that it's unspiritual to be seen so they go into hiding"*(.) He gave you the message so you can be a beacon of hope and change in your sphere of influence. When you dim your light, the people assigned to you can't find you. *"You are the light of [Christ to] the world. A city set on a hill cannot be hidden; nor does anyone light a lamp and put it under a basket, but on a lampstand, and it gives light to all who are in the house."* (Matthew 5:14-15)

When you understand that your influence extends beyond your role in church as a ministry leader or your status as an employee, you'll begin to positively change any environment you find yourself in because you're an heir of Christ. Your book is an extension of you and will reach places you've never seen before. Your words will bring life to someone facing depression or that's suicidal and praying for their miracle. Don't underestimate your ability to change atmospheres so that He can be glorified. It's a partnership. The way you live your life will be a demonstration of the power of prayer and submitting your plans to God while leaving the outcomes to Him. When your mind is set on empowering others, you will have less time to think about your problems and be solution driven. You're not saying that it doesn't exist, but you're trusting God to work it out for your good. When you mind His business, He takes care of your business. When you bear good fruit, you are honoring Him because you're living out the blueprint and being elevated to impart the knowledge and revelation you've been given. Protect your peace at all costs so that you are not lured in by individuals who want to bring confusion. Being misunderstood is part of the journey so make sure you stay committed to your Kingdom assignments. Think about your mission beyond the book and be teachable to learn new concepts as you grow.

Show up as a thought leader

As a thought leader you should always be ahead of the game. You set your own trend as you confidently lead the conversation in your community.

When you step into authorship while embodying thought leadership, you are positioning yourself as a personal brand. Think about how you can leverage the book once it's launched to your ideal reader and what the next step would be for them to work with you. *How do you want your author brand to be perceived? How do you want your dream client to feel after experiencing your services? Why did you write the book and how do you plan to leave a legacy with it?* I would encourage you to face any fears of intimidation so that you work through the emotions instead of running away from it. Many pioneers sabotage the success of a project before it starts because they believe it will fail based on past events. Thought leaders rise above their trials and follow God's standard for their book and business. You must believe that you're an expert first before becoming one. There are millions of coaches worldwide who have a certification and have not embraced their story or thought leadership. In my fourth book, *Unlock Your Voice Vol I: Breakthrough Strategies for Kingdom Women Who Are Called To Impact The Marketplace*, I outlined the power of unlocking your anointing, authority, and God-given gifts so that you can be equipped to serve in the marketplace.

I will now be sharing four action keys to shift your mindset as you transition from being a Kingdom author to becoming a thought leader:

Key one - Consistency is your superpower

Practice consistency daily in the small things so that you keep your momentum as you build your brand. Whenever you're experiencing a temporary setback, rest and reflect on how you can use the lessons as authentic content to show your community how you overcame it through your written posts or video content once you feel the release to share. Your transparency will give others permission to trust you and be themselves. Engaging with your community is key to growing your author business. Increase your visibility and speak about the mission of the Kingdom movements you're stewarding. When creating content is a lifestyle, you won't overthink showing up on a weekly basis to market your book or transforming lives with your powerful message on virtual speaking stages.

Key two – Tap into your originality

Tap into your authenticity as a leader and lead by example in the roles that have been assigned to you. Set the tone in how you conduct business and honor your word. Your credibility will rest upon your ability to convey the message the Lord has given you and modeling to others what it should look like. You should not compromise your originality because of people's opinions. Release the blueprints for your brand as you received it while spending time with God. This may result in you doing a series of live videos to break down your topic, creating personal quotes so that you don't have to copy and paste from others, or planning in-person networking events so that you can collaborate with like-minded visionaries. What He is calling you to do has never been done before and you need to be prepared for it. You can use the story points or concepts in your book as speaking topics when presenting it to your audience. When you implement this, you will release a unique sound that ministers to the hearts of many through your spoken words. I believe the hidden potential inside of you will be unlocked when you follow His instructions and the timing of launching your book projects or movements you will be birthing.

Key three – Fight for a cause bigger than you

When you're not fighting for a cause bigger than you, you'll follow the masses and merely exist. The fire within you should be reignited. You need fresh oil for this next season. There is a deeper meaning behind the 'why' of writing your book so that you can change the narrative. It could be to help the lost, empower single mothers, break the cycle of addiction, forgiving your abuser, or receiving your healing after abortion. He is calling you out of hiding so that you can be the voice to the voiceless. In most situations it's been prophesied to you which didn't make sense at the time. You can expect resistance when you address bloodline issues so that you're not conforming to the patterns of this world. If He chose you as a prophetic voice in the marketplace, obey. He will guide you in what to say and how to express it.

Key four – It's time for a rebrand

If you applied all the steps to launching your book, then schedule a mini-photo shoot to celebrate this milestone. If you have an allocated budget, get professionally branded photos and re-introduce yourself to your community. Repurpose the photos for your website, speaking portfolio, podcast graphics, and media features so that you represent your brand well. If there's aspects of your messaging or brand that no longer resonate with you, ditch the old so that you can make room for the new. If you've made it thus far, you have all the tools you need to live out your message courageously and to launch your book as a Scribe within 90 days. You will constantly be evolving as a brand and pivoting as an entrepreneur as you amplify your influence with your book. It will take boldness to move forward when faced with uncertainty, so I want to prepare and stir you prophetically for what's next.

JOURNAL PROMPT: Take 5-10 minutes to prophetically prayer journal and ask the Lord about the personal brand He wants you to build. You can read the word and play soft worship music in the background if you feel led to do so. Write down the action steps that you will implement over the next 90 days using the action keys above as inspiration to grow your author brand.

SCRIPTURE FOR REFLECTION

"Have I not commanded you? Be strong and courageous!
Do not be terrified or dismayed (intimidated), for the
Lord your God is with you wherever you go."
~Joshua 1:9

Part Three

CHAPTER EIGHT

Be Bold and Courageous

When I rebranded my online service-based business two years ago I was seeking the Lord for guidance because launching a personal brand takes grit and courage. You are going into territory where criticism from individuals who don't understand your assignment becomes a reality. If Jesus was persecuted while fulfilling His assignment, what makes us any different? The fear of rejection and the opinion of others keeps us in bondage so that we're unsuccessful in reaching our promised land. We don't have control over what people say to us, however, we have a choice on how we will respond. I've encountered many leaders who have reached burnout and were led to build their business from scratch because they were spearheading too many things. While growing my online author business I've been intentional to ask my community questions pertaining to how they perceive my brand message. Their feedback is always the same with the most recent response from a powerhouse leader in Australia doing amazing work in her community who wrote, *'I love your heart, your boldness and your tenacity.'* When I see my message impact nations it warms my heart and fuels me to keep on going. I've often asked myself where my boldness comes from, and I can honestly say it's because of my zeal for the Lord and the pit He saved me from when my own voice was unmuzzled.

As a senior flight attendant, whilst on duty for a repatriation flight in 2020, we heard about the news of a global pandemic and flew Frankfurt citizens back home when Covid-19 cases began to increase. On route back to Johannesburg, the pilot in command decided to fly over the pyramids in Egypt and as I peeked out of the window, I got a vision of how the Israelites were rescued out of captivity. After landing in Johannesburg our flight crew spent thirteen days in quarantine before we could return home to our families. I felt a paradigm shift and finished most of my chapters as I was flowing in my writing during my time in isolation. I was unlocked in lockdown. The supernatural encounter I experienced that day was the defining moment that shifted my perspective on transitions and leaving behind the' wilderness' mentality. The scripture that came to mind is recorded in Exodus 14:13, *'Then Moses said to the people, "Do not be afraid! Take your stand [be firm and confident and undismayed] and see the salvation of the LORD which He will accomplish for you today; for those Egyptians whom you have seen today, you will never see again.'* The giants you are facing may look intimidating from afar, but after closely inspecting, you'll soon realize that they have no power over you. I believe God wants many of you to receive this word today if you've been trusting for a breakthrough. He is your vindicator and if you've been betrayed, rejected, slandered, or treated unjustly, there is healing for you. Every time you failed and picked yourself back up again, you were courageous.

It cost you to finally have the confidence to be bold about your message. When people unsubscribe or unfollow your content in your community there is a sifting take place. They're not saying no to you, but your message that evolved and the re-invented you who is releasing a fresh sound. Not everyone will stay with you, and some are only passing through to get what they need from being assigned to you for a season. Don't hold on to people that God told you to let go of because it will be a distraction. My prayer is always that they would discover their destiny helpers wherever they go so they can be in alignment. If the Lord is leading you to step into unfamiliar terrain, then I want to challenge you to stand strong and not be moved by what you see in the natural.

'Then the Lord spoke to Moses, saying, "Send men to spy out the land of Canaan, which I am going to give to the sons of Israel. From each of their fathers' tribes you shall send a man, every one a leader among them." So Moses sent spies from the Wilderness of Paran at the command of the Lord, all of them men who were heads of the Israelites. Moses sent them to spy out the land of Canaan, and said to them, "Go up this way into the Negev (the South country); then go up into the hill country. When they returned from spying out the land, at the end of forty days, they came to Moses and Aaron and to all the congregation of the sons of Israel in the Wilderness of Paran at Kadesh, and brought back word to them and to all the congregation, and showed them the land's fruit. They reported to Moses and said, "We went in to the land where you sent us; and it certainly does flow with milk and honey, and this is its fruit. But the people who live in the land are strong, and the cities are fortified (walled) and very large; moreover, we saw there the descendants of Anak [people of great stature and courage].' (Numbers 13,1-3, 17,25-28)

When I meditated on this scripture, it was clear that the Lord entrusted Moses with an assignment to send out leaders with specific instructions to spy out the land in Canaan. They returned with fruit from the land and gave their findings to Moses. I can imagine that they were still trembling from the magnitude of what they saw while being gripped by fear. When you are not feeling courageous you must push through the discomfort and emotions that's pulling you back into familiarity. The land He has prepared for you may seem daunting because it looks different than what you're used to, but when you get to the other side of it, you'll discover that abundance and wealth was stored up for you. Those leaders that spied out the land forgot who they were and saw themselves as grasshoppers overthrown by their circumstances. Because of their disobedience, the congregation was complaining and wanted to go back to Egypt. A whole generation was wiped out because of their unbelief and murmuring. *What would you have done if you were in their shoes?* I could resonate with them because most of the assignments that the Lord has given me seemed impossible at the time. I was ready to tap out, but God. I couldn't see the full picture, but I knew that I would get the next steps while moving forward. And so will you.

Being bold about your faith as a leader in business is not for the faint-hearted because you must pray that you partner with the individuals who have similar values as you with no hidden agendas. When you have a burden to be a change agent so lives can be transformed, you choose His will over yours.

What failure taught me

We've all experienced failures at some stage of our lives and were faced with the decision to do it another way or move on. Failure is an event and doesn't define who you are. It taught me valuable lessons about myself and refined my character because it has always been one of my greatest fears growing up. Making mistakes is inevitable, but your resilience will stand out above the rest. If you launched an idea that failed, it only means you haven't discovered a successful formula yet. I stopped questioning God when I was led to do things in a particular way that made sense to others. We can save ourselves so much heartache when we follow His plan for our lives. Failure taught me to ask for help and to learn how to receive. Pride will make you figure it out on your own when you should be transparent about your struggles. Discouragement and disappointment are destiny killers, and it would be in your best interest to manage those emotions. Perfectionism was not going to save me because there is no truth in it. It prevented me from making decisions because I was fixated on what wouldn't work based on past experiences. If you're going to build a personal brand as a Kingdom author, you will need to be fearless when it comes to your assignment. If someone has broken my trust in a relationship, I learn the lesson and move on. It's not God's purpose for us to dwell on the pass and to walk with offense in our hearts. If you haven't forgiven yourself because of past failures, take this opportunity to do it right now. Don't let another moment go by before being open to receive love again, to be joyful again, to have your peace back again. Journal through those emotions so that you can come back into alignment. It wasn't your fault. There was purpose for your pain, but it's time to rest in Him so that you can flow again. The biggest lesson my two-year-old son has taught me is to forgive quickly and to just be. His favorite pastime is to play around in the house with a bunch of bulky keys that he hooks onto his pants modeling his dad. Sometimes he would misplace the keys, and it would take us hours to find it again, which was quite an adventure. We would eventually find the keys after sitting him down, explaining the seriousness of losing the keys again. We haven't solved his fascination and love for keys yet, but sometimes you must choose your battles and what you give your energy to. Make the memories now so that you don't regret not doing it later. Give others grace to make mistakes and let go of any unrealistic expectations you've set for yourself. As Scribes we're continually on a healing journey while writing and it's imperative to come out of agreement with any words spoken over you, saying that you're a failure because it's a lie. In hindsight, the failures I encountered led me to heaven's blueprint for my life because I surrendered my way of doing it. If you've veered off the path you were supposed to take, He is making it straight again, but you must be all in. When you embrace your inadequacies, you inspire others to be themselves. That's your greatest asset. Let your life be a living testimony to show your community what's possible when you trust God.

Your future looks bright, and you've overcome many life challenges. As you follow the steps in this book, my prayer is that you will accept the blueprint He has for your life, book, and business.

Called to the Nations

I can't recall ever uttering the words, 'I want to serve leaders from every nation.' I felt like Simon Peter where he was just minding his own business catching fish and the next moment, he was called and chosen to be a fisher of men. It's quite hilarious how it all unfolded for me. What I do remember saying while worshiping and laying in a posture of surrender on the floor was, *'Use me I'm available.'* The thing I grappled with the most was the way He called me to do ministry because it looked different to most five-fold leaders. It wasn't in a traditional ministry setting or to preach behind a pulpit every Sunday, and it took me a while to make peace with it. I followed His instruction and ventured into the marketplace to launch a prophetic hub for Scribes who are stewarding Kingdom movements. It makes sense now why I loved traveling and interacting with different cultures in my previous career as a flight attendant. I was ministering out of the country as the Spirit of the Lord led me to, in places like Dakar, Accra, UK and Washington DC by starting a conversation on the streets or in the hotel lobby. He was preparing me for what was coming next.

Your calling may stretch beyond your geographical location into the hemispheres you've dreamed of but have not physically ever seen. I consult with Faith-driven leaders across the globe from all walks of life. It's my Kingdom assignment in this season. Our small steps of obedience eventually unleashes us into our purpose. We're going to need a spirit of boldness if we're going to birth the books and build the brand according to God's design. It's not business as usual. Even with a step-by-step framework you must still implement it and live it out courageously. This is where the separation takes place between action takers and individuals who are overfed with information. If you're not availing yourself with an expectancy to 'go' where He is leading you, you'll stand the risk of being complacent and aborting your mission. The biggest battlefield of the mind that's fought daily is comparison. If another individual is celebrated in your presence, it's not taking away from who you are because you weren't created to compete against someone else. We have no business overexplaining ourselves or our next level moves to people who have no desire to please God. If you're being led to write for a global audience, don't hide your gift. It was given to you to show up boldly in the marketplace. You've apologized for being you for long enough and now it's time for you to rise above your circumstances so you can soar.

Here's seven faith pillars to live courageously:

Faith Pillar one: Favor is your portion

When you believe that you've been given the cloak of favor to do extraordinary things, you'll be unstoppable as you break new ground. Your worth is not tied to your failures and your determination will produce a harvest because of your faithfulness. You expect favor and it finds you wherever you go. It's not based on your works or hustling, but His ability to perform miracles in the midst of a famine. This is how you step into the overflow.

Faith Pillar two: He graced you for this

His grace is enabling you to finish well and to be fearless as a global visionary. You'll receive supernatural strength to resist the devil so that he can flee after submitting it to God. Release the control to try and figure it all out and trust His plan for your life and Kingdom brand. You are being established as a trusted voice because you worshiped your way through the chaos. When you are focused on heaven's agenda, your humility saturates a room. Your anointing can't be replicated, and your pour is valuable. Discern who is eligible to make withdrawals from you.

Faith Pillar three: Fund your Kingdom mission

Be bold about the mission He gave you to influence change in communities and don't be afraid to speak about your vision. You can use the books you write as a seed to birth local or international projects. As Kingdom financiers we're presented with the opportunity to partner with individuals who carry the Father's heart and sow financially into movements that transform lives.

Faith pillar four: Amplify your Voice

The spiritual realm is voice activated and when we release a sound there is a shift in the atmosphere. You must first find your voice so you can amplify it. Identify any fear that is muting your voice and obliterate the power it has over you. When you write using your authentic voice while walking in your authority as a Scribe, you give hope, encouragement, inspiration, and empowerment to others who need a lifeline. Interestingly, I was inspired to write my story when reading books of Christian leaders who challenged my thinking.

Faith pillar five: Maintain a positive mindset

Toxic relationships have the potential to stir up emotions in you that affect your emotional well-being. If your peace is compromised, you must be willing to distance yourself from unhealthy environments. Pray for a community that values spiritual and personal development. What you allow access to will either break your spirit or edify you to keep on building.

Faith pillar six: Be rooted and armored with truth

The fight is spiritual and in Ephesians 6: 11-12,14 we are encouraged to, *'Put on the full armor of God [for His precepts are like the splendid armor of a heavily-armed soldier], so that you may be able to [successfully] stand up against all the schemes and the strategies and the deceits of the devil. For our struggle is not against flesh and blood [contending only with physical opponents], but against the rulers, against the powers, against the world forces of this [present] darkness, against the spiritual forces of wickedness in the heavenly (supernatural) places. So stand firm and hold your ground, having tightened the wide band of truth (personal integrity, moral courage) around your waist and having put on the breastplate of righteousness (an upright heart).'*

Faith pillar seven: Stop disqualifying yourself

Everyone is saying, *'Why her'* and my question to you is, *'Why not you?'* *because you answer to God.* Be confident in your convictions and don't allow people to dictate what you're capable of accomplishing. He qualified you to build a six-figure author brand and to be present in rooms you only dreamed of. Be unapologetic about your growth.

In the next chapter you'll get my five-figure Bestseller framework on how to build a Signature Kingdom Author brand that honors God. If you've co-authored a collaborative book or desire to be featured in one, this blueprint will position you for exponential growth to amplify your authority.

JOURNAL PROMPT: Get in a quiet place and take 5-10 minutes to prophetically prayer journal and talk to the Lord. You can read the word and play soft worship music in the background if you feel led to do so. Pray for boldness and courage to execute the instructions He gave you. Be slow to speak, and quick to listen, and repent of any delayed obedience when spending time in the Secret place.

SCRIPTURE FOR REFLECTION

"You are the light of [Christ to] the world. A city set on a hill
cannot be hidden; nor does anyone light a lamp and put it under a
basket, but on a lampstand, and it gives light to all who are in the house."
~Matthew 5:14-15

CHAPTER NINE

Marketing beyond the Book

If you're an author and you don't have a game plan to market your book after it's launched, you're leaving money on the table. Marketing is the heartbeat of driving sales to your book business because it's your responsibility to increase your visibility if you don't have a dedicated team assisting you. Your goal should be to get your return of investment back on what you've invested in the publishing of your book. I felt led to create a collaborative network in my online author academy where Scribes have access to training courses inside of an online portal and extended marketing support with one of our partners to grow their author brand. You must keep your momentum and be creative in how you will spark interest for your book after the hype of reaching Bestseller status on Amazon, if that was part of your strategy. Usually, we create tailor-made marketing strategies for our clients that's a good fit for their audience and the type of result they're looking to get. Local in-person networking events and speaking engagements are the most popular ways to amplify your message. If your target-audience is ministry leaders in business, you can tailor-make your talks depending on what you want to achieve with your message. If you're not at this stage yet, you may want to come back to this chapter again before implementing this five-figure framework to skyrocket your author brand.

Whoever said that you'll only have to focus on publishing the book and the rest will sort itself out, is wrong. That doesn't exist unless you're paying someone to do it for you. Stay engaged with your audience and take them on the journey with you as they connect with your story.

You may fall into any of these two categories:

1. You've featured as a co-author in a collaborative book project and want to be the visionary author of your own book project.

Dream with me. There is absolutely nothing stopping you from being the visionary author of your own collaborative book project because you've already seen what's possible. If you're stewarding an existing business, then curating your own book while collaborating with other leaders can be an extension of your services. Right now, there are more than a dozen people in your community that would jump in if they resonated with the topic you're writing about. If you're committed to financing the Kingdom of God this should not be a free service because compiling, editing, formatting, and publishing a book costs money. Every featured author will contribute towards the project and the inclusions should be clearly stipulated in your contract. The vision of your book will draw individuals in to ask more questions, so this is not the time to play small. Once you've triggered an emotion with your own personal story, your ideal audience will have the freedom to ask questions as they see you as an authority in your field. I'm slowly transitioning from book coaching to one-on-one consulting in this season so that we can enhance the experience we give to our clients who need support in writing their book from a blank page to establishing a successful author brand that glorifies God.

2. You launched your solo book in 90 days and want to grow your brand by featuring as a co-author in a Multi-author book project.

One year after writing my first book I was presented with an opportunity to feature as an author in a collaborative book project with fourteen leaders which inspired me to amplify my message and expand my reach as a visionary author. If you decide to take this route you can use your contributing chapter to market your solo book and network with the co-authors in the book that you connect with. You must be a team player and teachable as you commit to the given timelines of writing your chapter and marketing the book on your platforms. This is a great opportunity for you to reach Bestseller status and grow your reach while connecting with dynamic leaders.

3. You've written a solo book and want to lead your own book project.

This opportunity is for my eagles and high achieving leaders who want to create impact in their communities through Kingdom collaborations while generating an income to fund missions. You value community and authentic relationships and are open to exploring new ways of growing your personal brand. If you want to steward a successful collaborative book you can partner with a publisher who has a proven method, so that you don't have to figure it out by yourself. I built my SOP's (Standard Operating Procedures) for leading a collaborative book from scratch and encountered many pitfalls you can avoid if you're considering becoming a visionary author. You don't have to repeat the same mistakes I made. Once you've curated your first collaborative book you can evaluate what worked and refine the steps that weren't working. When you invest in putting efficient systems in place, you will reap the rewards of the time you've put in.

I have a simple five-figure Bestseller framework that will position you to influence change in your communities.

• Vision and inspiration for your book

Get clarity around what you want the book to be about so that you can communicate it effectively to the featured authors. You are the visionary leader and should set the tone and expectations for the book project. Seek the Lord for direction on your book title, cover, and theme for your book and pricing structure. Decide if you're writing a journal, devotional, or compilation of stories so that you can create the outline for your book and use it as a template for authors to follow. Generally, the timeline for a collaborative book to be completed is four to six months, so create a checklist for yourself to stay on track. If the Lord impressed it on your heart to start, don't get despondent when you see everyone around you launching anthologies, because what you have to offer is unique. Remember, you're not competing with anyone that has a grand strategy with perfect graphics. You're staying in your lane and focused on your own assignment, executing it in the way you feel led to. God gives us the anointing and grace to complete our assignments. You must stand in your authority and not allow anyone to blur the vision.

• Alignment to book theme

There's a series of tasks that need to be set up before onboarding leaders that's the best fit for your book. If you have limited resources, you can start with a questionnaire to ask pertinent questions to interested individuals that are aligned to your vision and values. Depending on the investment you can decide if you want to have a quick interest call as a prerequisite to being considered. You need to be ready to give a full brief of the project on the call so that they can decide if they're committed to moving forward. Not everyone may be a good fit for that specific project. If you could delegate the administrative tasks, it would be ideal.

For the project to be viable and worth investing in, you should focus on a minimum of seven authors. Be mindful that depending on your word count per chapter, if you have more than fifteen authors the editing costs will be more expensive.

• *Rules of engagement*

Managing the expectations of the group is key so that everyone is on the same page. You can include those terms in your contract if you want to cover everything so that there is mutual respect. Should you be faced with any challenges, this is where your leadership skills will play a role in resolving unexpected issues. You will be stretched, so make prayer a priority. Avoid overcommitting yourself during this time to ensure you can serve with excellence. Communicate which platform will be used primarily for correspondence throughout the project. Think ahead and mitigate any possible timeline changes. Once you've set the price for your packages, don't compromise and undersell yourself because there may be hidden costs you never budgeted for. If you only have one price point, then you should communicate if you accept payment plans or only full payment. If you expect your clients to invest in your four or five figure service, then you should be open to making the same investments for your personal growth. My rule of thumb is not to ask for an amount you're unwilling to invest in yourself. When you are confident about your pricing, it shows.

• *Collaborate and celebrate*

Once you have everyone onboard you should work towards the goal of finishing your respective chapters before moving onto the editing and formatting phase. Make it fun and exciting by encouraging the authors as they write. If you have the capacity, you can meet weekly or monthly on zoom to work on creating a beautifully crafted chapter between 1500 and 3000 words. Flow in your gift of exhortation and celebrate one another. Create an environment to nurture relationships and be vulnerable so that your passions can be ignited as you write your powerful stories. Re-visit your checklist before starting your marketing campaign and assign a graphic designer to do your book cover and graphics before announcing the launch on social media. Distribute your marketing scripts and individual posters to the authors as you countdown the days to the launch. Once the book is live on Amazon the success of the book is a team effort, so ensure that the featured authors increase their visibility to promote the book on all platforms. Celebrate your wins and host your virtual launch party by going live collectively. You can also host an in-person book launch to promote signed copies of the book.

• *Rest and replicate*

Celebrate the success of your book launch. Take breaks in between and pace yourself so you're not burning out. Trust the process and the leading of Holy Spirit for the outcomes. You can now use this simple guideline and be someone else's destiny helper so they can fulfill the call of God on their life. Do it your way and use the blueprint He gives to you to add some personality. Every project will require a new approach so be sensitive to hear the voice of God during your quiet time.

The Holy Spirit spoke to my heart one day, asking me how I would feel if someone else would copy my ideas and make it theirs. There will always be copycats, but it shouldn't deter us from showing up authentically. There are people on an assignment to sabotage your vision because they've given access to the enemy, so discernment is key to who you're partnering with. However, I want to give you a new perspective after receiving a revelation for the times and seasons we're in. When an individual replicates your ideas, they won't be able to steward it with the anointing God has bestowed to you. As a visionary leader you will come across copycats that believe they can do it better than you. Their approach is not Kingdom-minded. Do it with excellence anyway.

When you encounter an individual who is offering a similar service to you there could possibly be a demand for what you were called to do. You are both walking out your unique mandates by serving different audiences so there is no need to feel intimidated because then it's a poverty mindset. This was my discovery when God's blueprint was unlocked in my life allowing me to build my author brand from my core identity and not my insecurities. This is the author community God instructed me to build that's founded on Kingdom wealth and wholeness. *What did He reveal to you?* Don't launch a book project or podcast because it's a popular trend, act because you're obedient. We need more Kingdom ambassadors that have the courage to lead groups and movements to edify the Body of Christ. Unfortunately, you do get instances where leaders have invested a huge amount of money and received a low-quality book or no book at all so the promise wasn't met. Their trust was broken and therefore they're skeptical to participate in future book collaborations because of the bad experience. There's always a risk involved if you're enlarging your territory, however, it should never deter you from being open to new opportunities with the right fit destiny helpers. Hope deferred makes the heart sick, so we shouldn't let disappointments keep us from reaching our prophetic destinies. Manage your emotions so that you can pass the test and move forward. You're not called to everyone and have no obligation to solve the problems of individuals you're not assigned to. When you narrow down your focus, you will have the time and energy to live out your purpose.

Purpose over Platform

Now that you have a simple framework of how Multi-author book projects work, you can step out in faith once you have the bandwidth to be a featured author or lead your own. The most powerful way to grow your reach and increase your book sales is to be a guest speaker at virtual speaking summits or a guest on a podcast that hosts your ideal audience.

Not every platform will be for you. In the past I've had many requests to feature as a speaker on a program as a motivational speaker on topics that I'm not passionate about or it's unrelated to my message. You may feel led to decline invitations that compromise your values or water down who you are. It's not worth it to be out of alignment. *What are your non-negotiables, so that you know what to say YES to?* Mark 8:36 reads, *'For what does it benefit a man to gain the whole world [with all its pleasures], and forfeit his soul?'* I believe that when you flow in your purpose that profit will follow. We can have all the highly esteemed accolades in the world and still miss God when it becomes an idol. The reason you were deployed into the marketplace was to take dominion for the Kingdom of God. The platform is only a medium for you to execute the vision. It's easy to get drawn in by what everyone else is doing around you because it sounds good. *Do others know what you stand for or are you blending in? Pause. Reflect.*

You don't have to convince anyone that you're a great speaker or author, but you do need to show up and shine in your zone of genius and eventually they'll see the gold in you. Trust your capabilities as you master your message. If at this stage you still need clarity on your target market, show up and serve because they'll be attracted to you organically as you amplify your voice. Your spiritual endowments will empower you to be bold as you powerfully share your story. However, you must put in the work and prepare for the platform while you're in your 'cave' season. The oil should always be burning in your lamp because you never know when the day will come that your gifts will make room for you. Be expectant for your harvest season. While you're waiting you should write the post, build your confidence, and finish the book. Stay within His rhythm so that you remember to rest. I thoroughly enjoyed my time writing these few chapters to you and I trust you will use it as a valuable resource as you grow your personal brand. This should be your go-to chapter once you've published your book or are planning to be a visionary author of your own book project. Get creative and plan your local book tour, go live to do a chapter reading and get visible on the international virtual stage. Marketing should be fun as you co-create with God. There is an abundant harvest waiting for you on the other side of stepping out of your comfort zone. He will give you the next steps when you make the first move and sow your seeds in fertile ground. You have been given all the tools to launch a successful book in 90 days. I challenge you to execute what you've learned against all odds because only you can make it happen.

Go back to the beginning of the book to check your progress so that you're not skipping steps. Sometimes you must read it more than once before it's remembered. Take your time to go through it and highlight specific areas that stand out for you and work through them. Remember to do the inner work before implementing any of the steps to finish your book. I'm rooting for you! In the final chapter you will be prophetically unleashed into your assignment as a Scribe so that you can be activated to influence nations with your gift of writing. As He unlocks your prophetic voice for a time such as this, you can expect a fresh fire to burn on the inside of you. God is raising up an army of faith-fueled pioneers who will write their books supernaturally over the next five years and I'm honored to be part of it.

JOURNAL PROMPT: Take 5-10 minutes to prophetically prayer journal and ask the Lord if there's a bigger picture beyond the book you're called to write. You can read the word and play soft worship music in the background if you feel led to do so. Write down what you see, feel, and hear and implement any instructions you receive.

SCRIPTURE FOR REFLECTION

"And Jesus answered them,
"The hour has come for the Son of Man to be glorified and exalted."
~John 12: 23

CHAPTER TEN

Unlock & Unleash the Scribe in You

Over the next five years we will encounter a shift that will propel many leaders into their God-given purpose so that they can embrace authorship. Books will be released supernaturally to individuals who are committed to growth and advancing the Kingdom of God. However, you must exchange the old way of thinking with a renewed mindset so you can view life and its challenges through the lens of Christ. I was pondering on how I wanted to end the final chapter of this book and therefore, I will allow Holy Spirit to flow through me through prophecy and exhortation.

"Supernatural provision is going to unlock doors of opportunity you could have only imagined. The Lord revealed to me that the reason prophetic Scribes were unsuccessful in birthing their books was because they're writing from the natural realm and have not tapped into the spiritual gifts He has given them to complete the assignment. As visionary leaders we have not stewarded our time and resources well, but expect God to give us an abundant harvest. We have grieved Holy Spirit because we've tried to fit him into our busy schedules and neglected to seek the Lord for direction concerning our families, businesses, and books we were called to write. During times of transition, we have disqualified ourselves from being used by Him because of our flaws and shortcomings. He is searching for vessels who are available with a heart to obey Him despite how they feel.

In this hour there will be a shaking in the earth that will test the faith of many as they are being ushered into His presence for a deeper intimacy. There will be no more compromise in doing what you were called to do. Those individuals who stand up for righteousness so that voices can be unmuted, will receive instructions from Him to execute immediately. There will be a roaring sound that will be heard across the nations, and this will signal the transfer of wealth to His people who have dedicated themselves to their Kingdom mandates. What you have branded yourself in the marketplace will change for His glory because you have not fully walked in your authority. You are His influencer and can't be contaminated by worldly systems and scripts. He wants to do a new thing in you as you occupy the land He is giving you. I see acres of land given to their rightful owners. I envision keys being released to doors that have been locked up for years that can now be opened. He is opening the treasure chest inside of you so the jewel in you can be seen. You will no longer be overlooked. He is pushing you to the forefront so that you can be a light bearer and place of refuge to the lost. Your words will be like balm on emotional wounds which have been infected for years so that healing can take place. He has given you dreams and visions that will be interpreted as you finish your book. You are the solution they've been waiting for. You are the blueprint. You are the gift. Stop thinking small because He wants more for you."

Your trials will serve as a catalyst to thrust you into the spiritual realm so that you're not led by the flesh. As you are being commissioned to start your journey as a Scribe, you need to give Him permission to work it out for your good on your behalf. Fear has no hold over you and when you give your YES you will be branded as chosen. Leaving the past behind you and moving forward towards your destiny. This is His promise when you partner with Him as a Scribe. I am sensitive to releasing prophetic words, but strongly sense that He wants a more meaningful relationship with you. He wants to give you rest while you're building the brand without striving or lack. This is your moment to step into it wholeheartedly.

There are three types of people you may resonate with:

The Visionary

You have an overflow of information that you've gathered over time, but have not implemented yet. You've stepped out in faith to some degree even though you're still seeking clarity on your dream audience and the tribe you're called to. As a creative you have many ideas, but desire direction on how to steward them. You're breaking out of your comfort zone so that He can unlock the hidden potential and dormant gifts inside of you. People pleasing and perfectionism affected your ability to flow prophetically and that's why the vision has not been executed. You've been destined to write many books that push others into their purpose, but have been facing countless distractions masked as good things. When you spend time in the secret place you will receive new strategies to move past the procrastination that was masked as a veil between you and your next level. He is redeeming your time so that you can get back into alignment. As you flow with the Spirit of God and take deliberate action, you can expect your prophetic vision to be RESTORED as you walk BOLDLY in your purpose.

The Explorer

You have a powerful message in your heart that fuels your passion to write and have launched a book or co-authored a collaborative book.

You've been a part of a few communities and sense the Lord is stretching you to increase your capacity. After experiencing many setbacks, you are committed to execute the new assignment He is giving you because your mission is to make an impact and reach more people. Your business was paused on purpose, so that you can be spiritually armed when going into battle. You're ready to ditch the old scripts and start afresh so that you can fulfill your prophetic destiny. As you transition you will experience resistance to stop building, however, the enemy won't succeed because He is giving you a fresh wind. He is rebranding, rebirthing, and reaffirming you as a Scribe as you make a new covenant to become who you are called to be. SURRENDER and trust that His timing is perfect.

The Dreamer

You're a prophetic person or an emerging prophet called to impact the marketplace. You dream big and think global whenever you execute your God-given vision. As a High achieving leader and successful entrepreneur you are not moved by accolades or titles, but pleasing God. The enemy attempted to mute your voice whenever you were close to breakthrough, and for a season you found yourself going back into hiding. He is sending you destiny helpers so that you can birth the movement that will break unhealthy patterns in your bloodline that have never been seen before. When you launch your book, you will stir gifts in others and awaken their dreams again. RELEASE your sound because you are His mouthpiece. The anointing that you carry will break through barriers and poverty thinking. Pick up your pen and partner with Him because He is unleashing the Scribe in you.

When the Lord amplifies your message, you will be tempted to go back to the wilderness, but He has already made your path straight and paved the way for you. You're making history because you refuse to settle for less. Don't let your books gather dust on the shelves because you believe it served its purpose. Breathe new life into the story you told because it's meant to reach someone else. Many leaders take their dreams to the grave, but that's not you. As you are sitting, lying, or standing up, whichever posture you're in, change it and move into a different position. Take prophetic action and take a step forward signifying that you are moving into His kairos time for your life. Make a commitment to yourself that you are making a comeback with your story so lives can be transformed. His favor is surrounding you.

I am eternally grateful that the Lord entrusted me to write this book in less than thirty days from a place of rest. If you asked me ten years ago what I would be doing with my life, it would certainly not have been what I get to do every day. I'm not the smartest, the most gifted, super talented, or eloquent person in the room, but I have a heart to please God with the resources I have in my hand while He does the rest. That's it. He transformed my life from being a little girl with an identity crisis who was overlooked, into a global visionary with a big dream influencing the nations.

You got a glimpse of my story, and I hope to share the rest with you when our paths cross or when we meet virtually again. **That's a promise**.

JOURNAL PROMPT: Get in a quiet place and take 5-10 minutes to prophetically prayer journal and talk to the Lord. You can read the word and play soft worship music in the background if you feel led to do so. Gratitude is an act of worship. Thank the Lord for all that He has done in your life and for who He is. Ask the Lord what He wants you to do with everything that you've learned, then obey swiftly. Keep those notes in a safe place after you've recorded the year and date in your journal.

Acknowledgements

Thank you Lord for giving me the supernatural ability to launch this book in less than 90 days from a place of rest. I dedicate my life to do Your work and to follow the leading of Holy Spirit. The prayer of my heart will always be 'Send me, I will GO' regardless of how I feel.

To my husband, thank you for watching the kids and for your words of encouragement during my writing process. Your heart to serve humanity inspires me. I love and honor you.

To Joshua and Jessica, one day when you're big you'll see the legacy mom left for you. Your future is bright and you're my greatest blessings.

To my spiritual mentor and accountability partner, Ps Chana Richards, thank you for being my destiny helper. My prayer is that your teachings will reach and transform nations.

To my family, thank you for your continued support. You play a pivotal role in my life and keep me grounded.

To my late father, if only you were here to witness the promises of God being fulfilled in my life. The seeds that were planted in me were not in vain.

To my clients and Kingdom partners from all across the globe, thank you for entrusting me with amplifying your stories and for your unwavering support.

To my editor, Cindy Rose and my publishing team, thank you for making this an effortless experience by assisting me in bringing this vision to life.

CONFESSION OF YOUR FAITH TO FULFILL YOUR DESTINY

Father, I stand in awe as I consider Your lovingkindness toward those that fear You, keep Your covenant, and walk in Your commandments. I come to You this day to proclaim that Jesus is the High Priest of my confession. I thank You for making a way for me to come to You.

Therefore, I come boldly before your throne with confidence as Your Son knowing that You hear my prayers and that Your heart is full of tender mercy towards me. I know that You are faithful to complete that good and perfect work You have begun in my life. I desire complete freedom from every sin that keeps me from my destiny.

I desire complete deliverance from generational accusations, bitterness, bondages, curses, and strongholds. Father, I desire to take back the ground in my life that has been controlled by the enemy of my soul. Like Jesus in John 14:30, I want to be able to proclaim that the prince of this world has no power over me and that I can walk as an OVERCOMER in this life through the righteousness I have in Christ Jesus.

PRAYER TO UNLOCK THE SCRIBE IN YOU

Father God, thank you for the gift of life and that I have the privilege to come boldly before Your throne of grace. I pray that You would activate any dormant gifts within me so that I can complete my assignment. Remove all hindrances that are distracting me from walking in my purpose. Forgive me if I have not been walking in obedience and birthing the vision You gave me. Use me as Your vessel as you unlock the Scribe in me to write supernaturally. I am leaving the past and old ways behind me so that I can become who You have ordained me to be. I pray this in Jesus Name, Amen.

PRAYER TO PARTNER WITH HOLY SPIRIT IN YOUR WRITING

Holy Spirit, I welcome You on this journey with me so that I can flow in my writing. I pray for a spirit of wisdom and discernment as I wait on Your guidance to outline my book. May Your will be done as you prepare the hearts of the people who are waiting on this message. I bring every unwritten chapter before You and ask that You would lead me and give clarity on how to communicate my story. I also pray for focus and mental strength to finish this assignment in Jesus Name we pray, Amen.

What to do next

1. We would love to hear your feedback on how you've been inspired to launch your book courageously in 90 days. Send an email to MeganCBruiners@consultant.com so we can celebrate with you.
2. We would love to gift you a free 20-min prophetic vision strategy call to get started on your book. Follow this link: https://www.wealthykingdomauthorsacademy.com/scribe-training or scan the QR code.

3. Schedule a complimentary 30-minute prophetic clarity call to discuss your book: https://calendly.com/megancbruiners/30minclaritycall

Here are a few ways you can get group or one-on-one support with Dr. Megan:

Group Cohort: The sixth round of our signature Cohort, Wealthy Kingdom Scribe 90 Day Accelerator, starts in February 2025 and enrollment is open. This will be an intimate group so that we can serve you with excellence and attend to all your questions. We will meet bi-weekly for X 8 Holy-spirit led sessions and it includes worksheets and accountability check in days via messenger. You also get a 3-month subscription to the Wealthy Kingdom Authors Academy with access to online courses, monthly coaching & writing formulas (Valued at $600)

You get two special bonuses when you join the Accelerator before **15 January 2025.**

- x1 60 minute 1:1 Prophetic vision Strategy call (Valued at $297)
- x1 60-minute consultation to discuss editing, publishing, or marketing for your book.

For more information on how to apply, scan the QR code below.

Mentorship for Prophetic Scribes: The Wealthy Kingdom Scribe Incubator is a $99 monthly membership to HEAL WHILE YOU WRITE and can be canceled at any time. Here's what you'll have access to:

- Monthly LIVE activation sessions covering course content (partnering with Holy Spirit in your writing, unlocking your Scribal anointing, the basics of building a Signature Kingdom Author Brand.)
- 60-minute Prophetic prayer journaling sessions every two months for spiritual, personal and professional development.

- Instant access to the Wealthy Kingdom Scribe online portal with training on Bloodline cleansing to break the pattern of generational curses in your bloodline so you can fulfill your destiny.
- Complimentary access to all paid challenges and Bootcamps (general access) over the next 6 months.
- Prophetic inner healing worksheets to position you to write your book as a Scribe.
- Support and accountability in a private community.

For more information, join our community here:
https://wealthykingdomauthorsacademy.com/incubator

One-on-one consultation: Become a visionary author of your own collaborative book project in 2025. Schedule a 30-minute interest call for all-inclusive publishing support here:

https://calendly.com/megancbruiners/30-minute-mastermind-collaborate

Schedule a 30-minute publishing consultation here:
https://calendly.com/megancbruiners/30min

Schedule a 60-minute prophetic journaling strategy call:
https://calendly.com/megancbruiners/30

Additional Resources

Grab a copy of my books on my website at www.meganbruiners.com. It is also available on Amazon, Amazon Kindle, Barnes & Nobles and at selected global stores. All the proceeds will go to a community initiative I've been tasked to spearhead in South Africa as we pay it forward to Faith-driven leaders that are changing the narrative in their sphere of influence.

Book me for Speaking

For virtual or speaking events (local or international) you can book a suitable time with me to present a tailor-made writing workshop for leaders in a corporate or ministry setting. If you're open to a purpose-driven collaboration, I'd love to do a talk on the concepts in this book at your book club, on a local city tour in South Africa, or in a panel-style interview directed at Faith-driven leaders.

Fill in this form to enquire.
https://www.meganbruiners.com/let-s-connect

Let's connect on socials:

Facebook: https://www.facebook.com/megan.jurd/
TikTok: www.tiktok.com/@megscribe
LinkedIn: https://www.linkedin.com/in/dr-megan-bruiners-0ab4a61a9
YouTube: www.youtube.com/@purposemid-wife3106
Website: www.meganbruiners.com

About the Author

Dr. Megan Bruiners, an authentic Prophetic voice, remarkable book consultant, distinguished as a 4x international bestselling author, a sought-after international speaker, Kingdom Publisher and the curator of The Unlock Your Voice Movement, takes center stage in the world of empowerment.

Her expertise lies in guiding visionary leaders and high achieving Faith-driven entrepreneurs to launch their book in 90 days while amplifying their anointing, authority and authenticity. She also unlocks their voices so they can live out their God-given message courageously as they steward their Signature Kingdom Author Brand that honors God.

Dr. Megan's illustrious path began when she completed her Master's degree in Tourism and Hospitality in 2015. The publication of her debut book in 2020, "Unmasking Purpose: A Guide To Overcoming Addiction And Discovering Purpose" unlocked this very year also saw her transition from a triumphant fourteen-year tenure as a senior flight attendant, even in the face of being retrenched. Her written words have since transcended borders, touching the hearts and minds of countless readers worldwide, igniting a spark of inspiration that propels them to unlock their boundless potential and live lives propelled by purpose. Hailing as a pioneering entrepreneur from Cape Town, South Africa, Dr. Megan stands as a beacon of change, resolute in her mission to shatter the chains of sexual sin, approval addiction, scarcity mindsets, and shame, while impacting leaders from across the globe. Alongside her husband of eleven years, David, they are raising two children of destiny.